BACKSTAIRS WITH

Upstairs,
Downstairs

BACKSTAIRS WITH

Upstairs, Downstairs

by

PATTY LOU FLOYD

St. Martin's Press
New York

Design by Jaya Dayal

Library of Congress Cataloging-in-Publication Data

Floyd, Patty Lou.
    Backstairs with "Upstairs, downstairs."

    1. Upstairs, downstairs (Television program)
I. Title.
PN1992.77.U633F56   1988   791.45′72   87-16345
ISBN 0-312-00996-8

First Edition

10 9 8 7 6 5 4 3 2 1

791.457
F

Contents

PART 1
The Portraits in the Parlor

PART 2
The Skeletons in Hudson's Pantry

PART 3

The Muse with Her Sleeves Rolled Up

PART 4

"And Which of Sarah's Pregnancies Was That, My Dear?"

Acknowledgments

I would like to acknowledge those who made this book possible: first of all, London Weekend Television itself—the producers of *Upstairs, Downstairs*—without whom this book would not exist; John Hawkesworth (producer), who gave me the copyright clearance to do the book, who read my manuscript, and who opened doors for me at London Weekend Television; Alfred Shaughnessy (script editor), who gave me his working notes for all the sixty-eight episodes, who guided me in the structure of my book, and through whose introduction I was able to work with Stella Ashley at London Weekend; Jeremy Paul (writer), who spent many hours walking me through the scripting process, who gave me several of his scripts and—not least—his working notes for the famous suicide episode; Rosemary Sisson (writer), for her notes and encouragement and time; Simon Williams (James), who shared with me the insights that gave him the key to playing James; David Langton (Richard Bellamy), for re-creating for me the atmosphere of the rehearsals; the late Joan Benham (Lady Pru), who told me lovely stories about the making of the series; Christopher Hodson (director); Cyril Coke (director), and the late Bill Bain (director); and Michael Smith, restaurateur and food historian, who told me about setting up Mrs. Bridges' kitchen, planning the menus, and supervising the setting of the table when Edward VII came to dinner.

At London Weekend Television I am indebted to the late Stella Ashley (drama organizer), who gave me all the production schedules, promotional synopses, stories of disastrous, late, and/or rejected scripts, and who opened many doors for me; the late Martin Case (casting director); John Emory (designer); Clare Daley (stage manager); Ken Ward (assistant stage manager); Bob Tuvey (property).

And my very special thanks to the late Audrey Colman, who gave me a desk in her office and retrieved for me the hundreds of still photographs from which I chose the pictures for this book. Without her patience and assistance this book would be utterly without photographs.

Prologue

The British television series *Upstairs, Downstairs* managed to do what no other series had ever even attempted—tell a long, long story without a book to go by. And did it with such style and wit and historical truth that it became:

- the most popular television series ever shown (one billion viewers, seventy countries)
- a classic whose videotapes sell alongside the great films of all time
- an elegy for an age, proclaimed by historians to be the best answer ever given to the question: What Happened to England?

Most of us, though, were slow in noticing all this.

The truth is, back in 1974, those of us tuning in to the opening episodes on PBS's *Masterpiece Theatre* weren't above being a little miffed. And there was plenty to be miffed about.

The trouble started with Episode 2. We wanted to see again the sassy under-houseparlormaid, Sarah, and the elegant Lady Marjorie and her husband. Instead, we saw an entirely new young man and woman named James and Elizabeth, and a Sarah who—behind our backs—had suddenly been transformed into a starving, consumptive waif. Nor—to judge from the looks James and Sarah were exchanging—was that the *only* thing that had been going on behind our backs.

From a snippet of dialogue we learned that, between Episodes 1 and 2, *three years* had elapsed! But as to what had happened in those years, we were left to guess.

Was it asking too much, we wondered, to be let in on the story?

In Episode 3 there was another new young man, named Laurence. And a love story about him and Elizabeth. This went on for two more episodes—then that was the end of Laurence.

Next, we moved on to the love story of James and Sarah. This, too, lasted for two episodes. Then that was the end of James (or so we thought at the time, not knowing that eight episodes later he would reappear).

Now, we met a *third* new young man, named Thomas. And watched another love story.

Though all of this was pleasant enough, it offered no riveting reason to tune in each following week. If we missed one love story, it seemed, we could catch the next.

What we didn't know then was that we were watching an edited version of the series. In bringing it to the States, Series I and II had been telescoped into a single series—twenty-six episodes into thirteen. From Series I, Episodes 2 through 9, and Episodes 11 and 12, had been deleted; and then from Series II, Episodes 1, 2, 4, 5, 8, 9, 10, 11, 12, and 13 were tucked in. (Series III and IV would proceed in proper order, uncut.)

Presented with this smorgasbord, we could be forgiven for thinking it was something we could sample at will—no need to sit through the whole dinner.

When we did begin to glimpse an order, a sequence of courses, we still did not suspect—not until after the writers did what they did to Lady Marjorie—that this progression was to tell, in the end, a story quite different from all those love stories. A story that would, in the end, bring us to tears.

This awareness of *another* story came to us only gradually, as the show (in Series II, III, and IV) became less episodic, developing continuing threads, and as we realized it was *not playing by the rules*. Not even by the basic one: Thou shalt not kill off thy leading lady in the second act.

Confronted now with the uneasy knowledge that these people at 165 Eaton Place did not inhabit some standard televised Never-never-land, we began to fear that if James got both legs shot to pieces in the war, he just might be left to sit out the remainder of the series in a wheelchair, or that if Gregory and the beautiful Rose didn't work it out together, she might spend all her days as a spinster and a servant.

If these people, then, were to be vulnerable to the same vagaries of fate as you and I, we could no longer go away for a week or so and expect to come back and find everyone safe, the house in order.

No, not even the house. And not even its ceremonies—like the serving of tea, whether in the morning room or in the servants' hall. The time was hinted at, in fact, when the house would not have room enough, nor the people time enough, for ceremonies of *any* sort.

And so we watched the Bellamys and Mrs. Bridges and Rose and Hudson and Daisy and Edward (and even Ruby!) with a growing sense of foreboding, a need to "look in on them." For time was catching up with 165 Eaton Place . . . just as it does with us in the real world.

As our loyalty grew, so also did our curiosity. How long, we wondered, would the series go on? And if it had to stop, why?

And who was the fairy godmother or godfather who had waved the magic wand and brought it forth?

When London Weekend Television sent us the answer *in person* —and it proved to be the lovely Jean Marsh, whom we already knew and loved as Rose, the head-houseparlormaid—it was like hearing that Cinderella herself, and not the Prince, had hosted the ball. It being so magic an answer, no one pressed beyond it to such mundane questions as: What *then*? Could it have been Cinderella who sent Lady Marjorie off on the wrong ship? Sent James to that hotel in Maidenhead? (Shame on her!)

Knowing, perhaps, how details can ruin the best of stories, none of her interviewers asked.

As soon as the final tape had run—and Mrs. Bridges had been led, bawling, out the servants' door for the last time—WGBH invited the stars and directors to Boston for a two-hour special (the so-called "wake"); fan clubs sprang up, clamoring for an immediate re-run, demanding to see the missing tapes they now knew existed; and articles appeared in newspapers and magazines, praising the series, telling us how it was breaking all records and how it was being dubbed into numerous languages.

But none of these articles answered any of the questions *I* wanted to ask. Who, for instance, was the cook who took those light and unsubstantial ingredients—those romances and melodramas and comedies of manners—and transformed them into an elegy for an age? And: How did they go about it? And: *Did they write down the recipe?*

Surely *someone* had jotted it down, I thought, but just to make sure, I wrote to find out—and was told that as a matter of fact *no one had asked.*

And so then *I* did. And for the next three summers, with Hawkesworth and Shaughnessy and Paul and Ashley as my guides, I was taken, step by step, through the five years they had spent putting the series together. In the years that followed I sorted and wrote, sorted and wrote (there were, remember, sixty-eight plays—not to speak of the stories that never reached the screen), sending it back occasionally to see if I were getting it right.

And this book is—as nearly as they and I could piece it together—the story of how *Upstairs, Downstairs* came into being.

Introduction

All the birds of the air
Fell a-sighing and a-sobbing
When they heard the bell toll
For poor Cock Robin.

—"The Death and Burial
of Poor Cock Robin,"
Mother Goose Rhymes

In Sweden, during the last year of *Upstairs, Downstairs,* the hour of vespers was changed—so that viewers would not have to choose between God and Hudson. It was even suggested, when the series ended, that a tolling of bells would not be inappropriate.

Over here, *Time* and *Newsweek* ran eulogies, PBS held a two-hour wake, and *The New York Times* hinted that the Carter administration was submitting to both houses of Congress a joint resolution declaring a day of national mourning.

Courtly mourning, of course.

Just who was being mourned was not, however, made clear. James? The Bellamys? The household? Or the series itself?

At a wake it is a good rule of thumb to have a corpse. During that two-hour vigil on PBS, the corpse was assumed to be the series. But at the more private wake afterward—dubbed the Boston Tea Party—the mourners latched on to Simon Williams, the actor who played James. "I was staggered," Bill Bain, one of the directors, said to me. "They reached out to clasp him, to reassure themselves that he was alive." A real witnessing; even reporters, sent to ask questions, volunteered testimonials. All for James.

James? One of the certifiable non-heroes of all time? Who bungled everything he put his hand to, mistreated his women, and went around whining that the times were out of joint?

A heady experience for Simon, who in England had been greeted on the streets with snarls and hisses. Why, over here, so many tears?

He was not alone in wondering. Many of us, the viewers, marveled that we could weep such tears for the likes of James.

No matter, we thought. When the obsequies are ended, when the tapes are rolled and stored, then there will be time—time for talk shows with the producer and the actors, time for postmortems in the magazines; then all our questions, both trivial and ponderous, will be answered. Why did they pack Lady Marjorie off on the *Titanic?* Why did they banish James from the show for almost a year? And why did all the reviewers fail to note that *Upstairs, Downstairs,* unlike other high-quality drama series, wrote its own story as it went along? (All the others had books to go by.)

We waited. But we heard nothing.

So, as happens when reality falls short of desire, fantasy moved in to fill the vacuum.

First, a long apocrypha by Alistair Cooke appeared in *The New York Times,* filling in the years since the moving van drove up to 165 Eaton Place.

Then, a myth arose. Having, like all good myths, the virtue of simplicity, it proclaimed that the series was conceived, written, and masterminded by Jean Marsh, the actress who played Rose, the head-houseparlormaid.

Within weeks, the gospel spread throughout the land. Jean Marsh was suddenly in demand on every talk show in the country and on many a college campus; as late as four years after the show had ended its run in this country, newspapers were still running big feature-length articles on "Jean Marsh, creator of *Upstairs, Downstairs.*"

The myth needed exegesis. It did not explain how Jean Marsh —or anyone—managed to write sixty-eight plays in five years. (Shakespeare, in a lifetime, managed only thirty-seven.) Nor did it explain who the "writers" listed in the credits were. Were they just window dressing—the way Joseph was—called in because of the doubters who might not believe that Mary had done it all on her own?

The myth, though it explained nothing, was perhaps more acceptable than the alternative—a committee. As if Tolstoy had doled out *War and Peace* to a stable of ghostwriters. "*You* do the opera scene; *you* do the Battle of Borodino; and *you*, the retreat to Smolensk. . . ."

All that aside, what kind of protracted hubris had prompted *anyone* to undertake a story that was to be five years in the telling? What if the network had said, "Enough!" just as Hazel was dusting off her typewriter and Lady Marjorie was embarking on the *Titanic?* And what about the casting? Did Simon Williams (James) sign away five years of his career on a shot in the dark? (No humor intended.)

All these things I wanted to know. And more. Why did the series speak so personally and so powerfully to us, on this side of the Atlantic, to whom its ways of life, its forms of speech, its symbols were as alien as the steps of a minuet?

But the gospel now was ended.

When, in the course of public obsequies, the mourning is ended and the legends have jelled, nothing is left but to go on a pilgrimage. . . .

I found I was not alone.

Yes, people did show up at 165 Eaton Place. From all over the world. Saying much about their determination and resourcefulness, because there is no Number 165. The house actually filmed was Number 65. But to avoid litigation from former tenants or their heirs, London Weekly Television pasted a "1" in front of the "65"—a precaution that very possibly caused more trouble than it saved, because for years the switchboards at LWT rang with questions from troubled fans who had gone to Number 165—and found it wasn't there.

Some of these pilgrims, standing there on the sidewalk, chatted about the "past." One woman—without so much as turning her head, just taking my presence and my interest for granted—said to me, "I never cared much for the way Virginia redecorated the morning room."

A young English boy, joining the others one day, had the good luck to see Lady Pru coming along the walk. (The late Joan Benham, who played Lady Pru, lived just around the corner.) He beamed at her, "Going to see Lord Bellamy, are you?" She tried to explain. But the truth was pallid stuff; *he* knew better.

Of the cluster of pilgrims there one day with me, my favorite was an elderly man, of slight build and patrician air, straight as his walking stick, who smiled and asked of no one in particular, "And is there honey still for tea?"

None of this is meant to imply that (1)65 Eaton Place is out-drawing the Changing of the Guard or the Tower of London. But in time, who knows? Wouldn't you swap a look at Henry VIII's armor for a glimpse into the morning room?

Myths and pilgrimages are all well and good. They feed our wonder. But not our curiosity.

I decided to write and ask some of the questions I thought the reviewers and reporters should have been asking. Sending the letters to those whose names I remembered from the credits, addressing them "Care of London Weekend Television, London, England," I dropped them in the mailbox and went home to wait, feeling about as hopeful of a response as if I'd put them in a bottle and tossed them out to sea.

They wrote back! Said they would be pleased to talk with me. Said they had been hoping someone would get around to asking the right questions. Even if it turned out to be a housewife.

I went to England. And there, over the next three summers, they recreated for me those days when John Hawkesworth separated the upstairs from the downstairs—and saw that it was good.

Now, like Lazarus, I have come back. To tell you all.

BACKSTAIRS WITH
Upstairs, Downstairs

Setting up for Episode 1.

The household at 165 Eaton Place.

Sarah, applying for post of under-houseparlormaid, is sent to servants' entrance. (Episode 1, "On Trial.")

Sarah exposed. (Episode 1, "On Trial.")

Wedding Bells. (Episode 3, "For Love of Love.")

Guess who's coming to dinner? (Episode 7, "Guest of Honor.")

". . . and guess who's coming for dessert?" (Episode 7, "Guest of Honor.")

The christening party. (Episode 8, "Out of the Everywhere.")

Elizabeth and her benefactor. (Episode 11, "The Fruits of Love.")

When trouble comes, Sir Geoffrey's sure to follow. (Episode 11, "The Fruits of Love.")

Farewell party for Sarah and Thomas. (Episode 12, "The Wages of Sin.")

The end of an era—the death of King Edward VII. (Episode 13, "A Family Gathering.")

PART 1

The Portraits
in the Parlor

1

Once upon a time, in a land called England, there lived a very great actress, so great that she always got very grand parts. Like Electra. Or Antigone. But she, alas, wanted to play comedy.

Season after season, while other actresses got parts in farce and slapstick and sexy revues, she went on doing the same old thing—Aeschylus, Sophocles, Shakespeare. She was very sad.

One day she and another actress were being sad together beside a swimming pool in the south of France, when they had an idea: They would write a comedy of their own to act in.

And so they did.

And lived happily ever after.

Or one of them did.

The other one, the tragedienne . . . but that story must wait.

Meanwhile . . . by the pool, the tragedienne (Eileen Atkins) and her companion (Jean Marsh) discovered they had come from the same side of the landing; i.e., their parents had been in domestic service. Here, they decided, was the lode of their comedy.

And why settle for just one? Why not a series?

Because they were convinced that, being women *and* actresses, they would get short shrift at the networks, they took their idea to a producer Ms. Marsh had once worked for—John Whitney, a partner in a company that invents, buys, packages, and sells ideas to television networks.

Whitney said to her, "I can't do it; I've just taken on the job of managing director for Capital Radio. Let's talk to my partner."

The partner was John Hawkesworth.

And so it was that in the summer of 1969, a company called Sagitta Productions (which prepares and sells ideas to networks) bought an idea about *two servant girls in a country house* in Victorian England—an idea that would prove to be light-years away from the series in which a young man named James Bellamy would come to his death in a Maidenhead hotel.

2

Was this the face that launched a
thousand ships?

—Christopher Marlowe, *Dr. Faustus*

"It's purely for idiots who don't read much, if they read at all. And they won't read more than a page. So you do it very simply: 'This show is going to be epoch-making; it's fraught with dramatic possibilities' . . . all that. I'd learned how at J. Walter Thompson, writing commercials for lavatory paper—'This napkin paper is going to make you glamorous and beautiful . . .' "

This, from John Hawkesworth, at our first interview, describing the sales proposal he and Whitney eventually submitted to London Weekend Television.

Prior to this interview with Hawkesworth, London Weekend had given me a copy of that proposal—the very first bit of *Upstairs, Downstairs* put into my hands.

"What I expected," I said now to John Hawkesworth, "was a glimpse of the Muse, in her pristine state."

"Not at all. Just an ad for lavatory paper."

The proposal opened with this description of the Edwardian setting:

> Never since Roman times had the Western world enjoyed such an orgy of pleasure. . . . Young bloods drank to their mistresses sculptured in ice cream. . . . It was almost conventional for the rich Englishman to have his little stucco love nest in St. John's Wood. . . .

And continued with a cast of characters that might have been more at home at Peyton Place than at Eaton Place:

RICHARD BELLAMY—Divorced . . . remarried . . . has a mistress in St. John's Wood. A matter of continual speculation is his relationship with his butler, Hudson, of whom he is fonder than anyone else in the world. . . . He has other *less conventional vices and strange appetites* [italics mine], which make him vulnerable to a blackmailer.

GAIL BELLAMY (his wife)—An actress and a dancer, one of the first to become respectable through marriage. Her wildness and beauty made her famous in her youth, and her name was linked with the Prince of Wales . . . tough and ruthless, a born intriguer with a network of spies that keep her informed. . . . She has many lovers but conducts her affairs with tact—and usually to gain a foothold in an important camp.

ROSIE MIMMS—Gail Bellamy's most trustworthy ally. They have a great deal in common. [She will be wildly jealous of Mary Buck], not realizing it is the terrible jealousy of a lover. [Only one hint of the Rose we will know]: Her speech, manners, and outlook . . . put her a cut above the other servants.

HUDSON— . . . drinks his master's port and smokes his cigars . . . likes to give the impression that all decisions are made jointly by him and Bellamy . . . has a vast fund of risqué stories.

MRS. BRIDGES— . . . has a vast curiosity about everything to do with sex . . . has a vitriolic tongue . . . and is constantly feuding with someone. When she is on speaking terms with Hudson, they like to indulge in bawdy gossip and spicy reminiscences. . . . In her off-duty hours she disappears into her room and tipples, usually alone.

Only James and Elizabeth are recognizable:

> JAMES—Intelligent, attractive to women . . . a complete boun-
> der. A spoilt young man with too much money . . . constantly in
> trouble.
> ELIZABETH—Suffragette, pacifist, Edwardian equivalent of a hip-
> pie. [One overriding difference from the Elizabeth of the actual
> series]: She has no time for romance.

Then this surprise:

> MARY BUCK—*The central character of our stories.* [Italics mine.]

Who, you might ask, was Mary Buck? Well, we the television
audience never met her; the role was especially created for Eileen
Atkins, the Swan who wanted to play in a comedy. Of which, more
anon.

The titillating possibilities of this ménage are made clear, as
"with a preponderance of females below stairs . . . love affairs of
every sort were unrestrained . . . when the Bellamys go abroad . . .
strange and scandalous things sometimes go on in the empty house."

A surprise of a different nature: The upstairs cast in no way had
equal billing. The series was to be about "domestic servants, below
stairs," centering on Mary Buck and Rosie Mimms.

The tone of the proposal changes from the voice of the huckster
to that of the historian when describing the household's daily ritual:

> The day started at 5:00 A.M. for the junior servants. The cookers
> had to be cleaned and lit and blackleaded; the boilers stoked; the
> front steps to be scrubbed; breakfast cooked for the upper servants;
> the gentlemen's boots to be cleaned and the bootlaces ironed. . . .
> At nine o'clock came the first ceremonial parade of the day. The
> family all being present, the servants filed in and knelt while the
> master read a prayer from the family Bible.

The description goes on through the day "until the last glass was put away and the last guest gone."

Like all documents, the proposal had its small print. At the very end, it states, "It is not intended that the series should be mere kitchen-maid romances, but serious dramatizations by the best writers available and made to the highest possible standards."

Except for the small print, the package bought by London Weekend Television dangled the same old prurient promise—that wheresoever it might wander, upstairs or down, it would linger longest in my lady's chamber.

Beware of Greeks bearing gifts.

—Virgil, *Aeneid*

L ondon Weekend Television didn't know it, but they had
bought a Trojan horse. Imagine their surprise when they opened it
and out stepped not the philandering Bellamy nor the music-hall
singer Nell Gwynne wife nor the sinister butler but the thoroughly
upright son of a parson, the impeccable daughter of an earl, and a
Bible-quoting butler.

Gone were the German mistress, the conspiring Rosie, and the
tippling cook—not to speak of the hanky-panky between the butler
and his master.

These changes are the work of Alfred Shaughnessy, the script
editor for *Upstairs, Downstairs.* "I wanted the best script editor in
the country," Hawkesworth told me, "and that's Freddie."

Shaughnessy explained the changes to me. "I didn't want the
demimonde of Edward VII's amorous intrigues; I wanted a politically
well-placed family, so that we could let the viewers live through
the dramatic events of the period, as they affected the Bellamys."

He wanted to make it possible to "draw parallels from reality"— as in the marriage of Alfred Duff Cooper to Lady Diane Manners. There had been several such marriages in British political history, "where a politician—an ordinary 'mister,' had married the daughter of a great noble house, and had been slightly patronized by them. So, it gave us this thing of a man not quite able to be a free agent because of the pressure of his wife's powerful, influential family."

In a story about Mary Buck and Rosie Mimms?

Well, that was another change—the upstairs now had achieved equal status.

So, the name of the series had to be changed too. *The Servants' Hall*, the original title, would no longer do. Nor would *Two Little Maids in Town*. They took the new name from a nursery rhyme.

> *Goosey, goosey gander,*
> *Whither do you wander?*
> *Upstairs, downstairs,*
> *And in my lady's chamber.*

Being now the story of an entire household—and of a respectable household at that—the stories can move out of the back streets and onto the grand boulevards of history.

In Shaughnessy's early notes he even presages how Richard's political downfall can, through these changes, come about: "Because of his marriage and the patronage of his wife's family, Richard has suppressed his feelings for the Liberal cause . . . and his tragedy will be that he will, therefore, miss high office and power when the Liberals sweep the board."

Cloaked in an innocuous concern for economy, Shaughnessy also makes a subversive and reactionary suggestion, but one that was to set *Upstairs, Downstairs* squarely against the stream of the time— that is, to do the series on tape, not on film. With those old-style, stationary, studio video cameras that required three-sided sitcom sets. *Low budget.*

To avoid the expense of filming [Shaughnessy wrote] . . . I am
in favour of keeping the whole thing in the one basic setting. . . .
If the playwright's craft is brought to bear, there should be no need
ever to see a London street or a coach-and-pair. . . . Noel Coward
showed us the whole of Queen Victoria's funeral in *Cavalcade* through
the eyes of the Marriott children, leaning out of the nursery window.
So, please let's remember that television is *electronic theatre and not
second-rate film.* [Italics mine.]

A brave and backward step, for video was already a poor relation
to film, considered fit only for soaps and sitcoms. Television drama
was now modeling itself upon cinema, turning its back on the
limitations of video and of theater. And on that sacrosanct medium
of the theater—the word. With film the writer shared the act of
creation with cameramen, directors, and film editors. Films could
be created in the cutting room as well as at the typewriter. Not so
with televised theater.

For a brief, glorious while, Shaughnessy reversed all that. Of the
sixty-eight episodes of *Upstairs, Downstairs*, only five involved major
filming: the shooting weekend at Somerby Park, the fox hunt at
Somerby Park, the servants' holiday at the seaside, the train-station
scene in the war series, and the holiday in Scotland.

Here, then, was the chance for the writer to regain his lost
primacy. "It was a chance, in a new form," Jeremy Paul, one of the
principal writers, recalls. "It was related to the novel, to film, and
to theater—but new to itself. It can't move around, like film; can't
be introspective or subjective, like the novel; can't have episodes
without drama and things happening, like the novel; can't meander
off, like film or the novel. It has to be honed down, to play only
the center of a scene, to grab the essence and move on.

"Yet its positive side emerged from all those things it can't be."
Because of those immovable studio cameras, the writers turned to
longer scenes, to all the age-old, abandoned devices of the theater
—especially, the word. Later, because of the forbidding length of

the series, they would turn to the devices of the novel—such as the leisurely probing of character.

All blessings, it is said, are mixed. As the series went on . . . and on, the limitations of that small and charming set known to us as the morning room became a great bête noire, prompting one sorely challenged director (Christopher Hodson) to remark that the series should be subtitled "Twenty-Seven Years in the Morning Room."

That video's limitations were part of the secret amalgam of *Upstairs, Downstairs* no successor, alas, has seemed eager to learn.

4

*Between the conception
And the creation*

. . . .

Falls the shadow.

—T. S. Eliot, "The Hollow Men"

Now, with a name to call itself, a producer, and a script editor, the series moved to London Weekend Television's offices on the Thames. More specifically, Hawkesworth and Shaughnessy were assigned to an office—together. There, like two great Vulcans, they began to hammer out the world of 165 Eaton Place.

Soon that office resounded with the rumblings of creation—and of their differences, which were legion, protracted, and unrestrained. Could the Muse survive such a fray? London Weekend feared not and, having a vested interest in the outcome, decided to offer them separate offices.

"Separate offices?" they asked. "Whatever for?"

So they were left to their ways. Fortunately. Because there are those who believe that the electricity created by those two minds was the spark that made two and two come out five.

Their first order of business, on this first series as on the four succeeding ones, was to decide how things would end. (They never just stopped at the end of the season, as other series do.)

Series I—a wedding or a funeral? If a wedding, how about a Cinderella wedding—James and the under-houseparlormaid? Or Elizabeth's? Or perhaps a funeral—Edward VII's?

Next, Hawkesworth and Shaughnessy turned to the fate of the other characters in the year's series. Would Sarah get sacked? Married? Pregnant? And in what order?

Last, they would discuss what would happen along the way. Richard to the Admiralty? Alfred to the gallows?

Shaughnessy would take these ideas, go away, and write thirteen story outlines.

With these outlines they would meet again in that office—and again the creative fur would fly.

When it settled, the writers would be called in and assigned the stories.

That was the idea, anyway.

Between the idea and the reality . . . lies our story.

Series I. The first six outlines had been assigned to writers, the first script written . . . when they lost their leading lady.

Remember Eileen Atkins, the tragedienne in search of a comedy? Here she was, with the custom-made comic role of Mary Buck, the proposed central character of the series—and what does she do? She returns to the grand and queenly roles she had fled. To Queen Victoria in *Vivat, Vivat, Regina*.

What do you do when the actor playing Falstaff quits and you can't find another fat man?

If you're the script editor, you keep your pencil sharp.

Hawkesworth and Shaughnessy resolved the problem back-side-to. They did away with the part altogether; Hawkesworth hired a new actress (Pauline Collins); Shaughnessy studied her; and an entirely new role was created.

Exit Mary Buck. Enter Sarah.

But they planned to get rid of her in Episode 3. This was the story they wrote for the event (*Board Wages*, which we in the States never got a chance to see): One night when the Bellamys and the older servants are away, the younger servants stage a mock soiree. Dressed up in the Bellamys' clothes, drinking the Bellamys' gin, they are having a high old time in the morning room, aping their betters, when James returns home unexpectedly. Instead of being outraged, he joins the fun—acting as their butler, even serving them the Bellamys' champagne. The charade ends with James following Sarah upstairs when she goes to remove Lady Marjorie's clothes . . . just as the moment is turning tender, it is shattered by a loud crash from downstairs. Rushing down, they see the Alfred, the footman, slinking away from a spreading puddle of splintered crystal and spilled champagne. Curtly, James orders Sarah to clean it up. In his arms one moment, on her hands and knees before him the next, wiping up the bubbles of make-believe—she goes upstairs to pack her bag.

Exit Sarah.

Unforgivable! Because by the time the episode was taped, everyone could see that Sarah was, in fact, going to be the hit of the series.

So an urgent note soon appears, handwritten, in the margin of Shaughnessy's drafts: "Bring Sarah back!" (They come up with a story in which Elizabeth and James, on a round of social work, find her in a soap queue in the East End.)

Not long after this, *another* note will appear in the margin: "Sarah is back with us—but she must be sacked."

Poor Sarah. With all those pregnancies still to come.

The loss of Eileen Atkins and the ongoing saga of Sarah show how the *Upstairs, Downstairs* Muse *really* worked.

5

*They sought it with thimbles, they
sought it with care;
They pursued it with forks and hope;
They threatened its life with a railway-
share;
They charmed it with smiles and soap.*

—Lewis Carroll, "The Beaver's Lesson"

Consistency. Hawkesworth and Shaughnessy were indefatigable in pursuit of it.

To make sure it didn't elude them, they planned to limit the number of writers to three or four, whom they could closely oversee.

But no sooner was the contract with LWT signed (1969) than Hawkesworth was told that, because of scheduling, he had *five* weeks to come up with six scripts.

Nothing to do but to hire six writers, one for each script, tell them the story they were to write, give them a set of guidelines—and then hope the styles would not veer from Ibsenesque to Kafkaesque.

No such luck.

When the scripts came in, "Some were ponderous, full of high sentence, reciting great tracts of history at you," Shaughnessy recalled. Others looked on history with a lascivious eye, "all erotic and depraved." And then there were those who "started building up this below-stairs hell—rats and cockroaches and grime—making a sociological drama out of it, and I had to say, 'This isn't Maxim Gorky; we're not doing *The Lower Depths.*' "

Consistency. Once more, Hawkesworth and Shaughnessy walked the writers through a tour of that lost world of downstairs, where no cook would stoop to scrub a potato or scour a pan.

They had already worked out a set of guidelines—which, in fact, had been explained to those first six writers. As nearly as I could reconstruct them from their notes and our interviews, the guidelines went like this:

1. The series was to be a story of a tightly knit, supportive household, bound by blood and by service, where everything that happens to one affects all, upstairs and down.
2. Each episode would have an upstairs plot and a downstairs plot.
3. Each episode would be complete in itself. (A first for a drama series. Most of them, being based on novels or biographies, just stopped in midstream. Take *The Jewel in the Crown*, when we find Sarah Layton being undressed at the end of one episode, and pregnant in the next. Only sitcom writers were expected, week after week, to deal with a beginning, a middle, and an end.)
4. Each episode was to be a drama in three acts. (Also a first. And a nicety lost on us over here, because PBS ran them with no breaks, and commercial television reran them with more than three.)
5. Each episode would be in a traditional genre of the stage: a drawing-room comedy, a satire, a melodrama. (Another first. It warned the writers that *consistency was not to be attained by falling into formulas.*)
6. Each episode, while complete in itself, would also have a careful continuity with the one preceding and the one fol-

lowing. If done well, this meant the series could tell a story larger than its parts.

7. The stories would go forward in time. (Unlike *M*A*S*H*, for instance, where their Korean war dragged on longer than the real one.)

8. The characters would develop. (Radical. Did Archie Bunker outgrow his bigotry? Or, conversely, did his bigotry ever grow malevolent? No, he remains forever the bigot, but forever harmless. Once television characters are established they all too often congeal, as though set in concrete.)

9. The series would have *no* leading roles. Though each member of the cast would be given one story in which he played the lead, he would in others play only a supporting role—or *none at all*. (This innovation, meant as an economy measure, became the show's salvation; in Series II, when James left the show; in Series III, when Lady Marjorie, Elizabeth, Sarah, and Thomas—all at once—said "Enough!" Later, still, however, it would prove to be a straitjacket: When the story begins to find its chief metaphor and momentum in James, Ruby must have her day. By that time, though, fans were more than happy to see her have it.)

10. The money saved by using only part of the cast in any one show would be used to bring in guest actors for each episode.

11. The writers were not to try to turn videotape into second-rate film; they were, instead, to explore its potential for imitating the theater. To wit:

    a. There would be a minimum of sets. Almost every scene in every story would take place inside the Bellamys' house.

    b. To avoid the need for so many sets, the stories would play on dialogue, and on long scenes.

    c. There would be no action sequences. Action would come through interplay of character.

    d. They would not try to create a sense of drama through resorting to special effects, music, or noise.

to have been largely implied, deduced from bits of circumstantial evidence, perhaps a mislaid opera program or the torn fragments of a letter pieced together by the servants. Mannerly. Discreet.

When the script came in, it missed on all counts—and it was late. "Four days to the deadline, too late to get another writer," Hawkesworth told me. "One of those moments when you have to make a decision. Freddie and I got together and we decided to chuck it and that I'd write one myself."

And he did. But four days proved too few for patterning the subtleties of such a formalized affair; what was to have been oblique became direct.

And that is how it came to pass that Lady Marjorie appeared before the cameras in her lover's bed—a state of affairs more unthinkable in hindsight than at the time, when they were still hammering away at the writers, trying to come up with that decorous style that was to become the show's hallmark—understated, unexplicit, observing always an aesthetic distance, whether in bed or in the trenches.

Even in this rush job Hawkesworth plants a theme that, with many variations, will be played on throughout the series and that will, with tragic irony, lead to Richard's political ruin.

Thanks to all this massive rewriting, only two of the stories, when finally taped, appeared (to the cognoscenti) really incongruous—the four-day wonder, *Magic Casements*, and *The Swedish Tiger*, in which poor Sarah, seduced by a houseguest's valet, burglarizes the morning room.

How did the writers feel about all these unprecedented guidelines? Well . . . the attrition rate was high.

First of all, though they were prepared to accept a certain set of givens and unspoken no-nos (just as Mary Tyler Moore was never, ever allowed to give a successful party), the writers were not accustomed to being handed the story they were to tell—except when adapting novels and biographies. Some thought it reduced them to hacks; some felt it constricted but did not throttle their creativity; others—remembering that dramatists from Aeschylus to Archibald MacLeish have had an affinity for second-hand plots—warmed to the challenge.

The writers who responded best were those with no illusions about how many story ideas there are in the world. "Eleven?" I suggested to Jeremy Paul (one of the principal writers).

"That many?" he replied.

Yes. Just a few. Reduced to a two-or-three-sentence outline, all stories turn into these same few hackneyed tales, just as Chaucer's bawdy *Merchant's Tale* and Tolstoy's moralistic *Anna Karenina*: both spring from the same basic story of The Young Bride and The Old Bridegroom.

"To work with these basic story ideas, there has to come a fascination with 'What is a cliché?' " Paul said. "Rose and her Australian sheep farmer—that was the old story of The Maid and the Stranger. The first thing is to *recognize* a cliché; then you have to meet it head-on, say, 'Well, *that's* what is expected now, so *that's* what we're not going to do.' "

Another of the writers who warmed to the challenge was Rosemary Anne Sisson. "John and Freddie gave us the skeleton of our stories, but after that they gave us our creative freedom; they let us put our own particular face and flesh on it. And we could always refer back to them—they were receptive to our suggestions."

The writers were not handed just one story assignment, however, but *two*. Both the upstairs *and* the downstairs had to have a story. Sisson, for one, didn't mind. "I like having a strong subplot. In fact, I prefer two." Paul had reservations. "Occasionally the stories worked terribly well in juxtaposition" (as when James, running for a seat in the House, shows compassion for the returning soldier, and in his own house quite ignores the plight of Edward), "but sometimes they made for too tidy a structure, too neat a parallel." (As when, upstairs, Hazel learns her aviator-lover has been killed in France, while downstairs, Rose learns her Australian fiancé has been killed.)

The rule that *did* upset the writers was the one allotting them only a part of the cast. "And not always the ones they wanted!" Hawkesworth recalled. " 'What's Sir Geoffrey doing in my love story?' " they'd ask.

Paul felt it was one of the things that kept the series from going flat. "It made us juggle the pack; it stimulated invention." In one story, he recalled, he found he had no one for Rose to confide in—except Edward, "and none of us at that time had established any kind of relationship between those two; so I had to set one up, create a bit of closeness, so that she could confide in him."

"And the times we had a character we didn't want!" Sisson recalled. "But because he had been contracted for months ahead, we *had* to use him." "And not just dropping in for tea," Paul added. "If I'd gone to rehearsal and seen a fine actor like Raymond Huntley [Sir Geoffrey Dillon] just saying 'Thank you very much,' I'd have been ashamed. So, I'd work very hard to give him a worthwhile scene."

"That 'worthwhile scene' often determined the fortunes of the family," Shaughnessy told me, "disillusioning as that may seem in terms of artistic creation." Remember when Richard and Marjorie were going to lose the house? Well, that came about because Shaughnessy found himself with Sir Geoffrey Dillon on his cast list.

When Series I was finally wrapped up, what had been established? In terms of continuity, not much, largely because of that practice of giving each of the twelve regulars a story of his or her own. In showing characters developing with the passage of time, not as much as they had hoped for. And the basic story lines leaned heavily on lonely and/or lovelorn servant women.

But in other areas the series was securely on its way. It had established a style all its own—witty, literate, reticent—belonging to it and to no other show. It had created an entire gallery of highly individualized characters. It had broken new ground in combining social history and drama.

And above all, it had introduced a world as alien to us as a Gregorian chant to a rock festival; a world of hierarchies where the cook and butler are served at table downstairs just as the Bellamys are served upstairs; a world of ordered civilities and ceremonies; a world where people behaved differently from you and me.

It had planted themes inherent to that world, themes that could—and later would—carry weightier tales than those of forlorn loves of parlormaids. Old-fashioned themes, such as responsibility, loyalty, standards.

6

I do not like thee, Dr. Fell;
The reason why I cannot tell;
But this I know, I know full well:
I do not like thee, Dr. Fell.

—Mother Goose Rhymes

I n all good fairy tales, this would be the time to hear that "they lived happily ever after." But in our story it was not immediately to be. Enter the Drama Controller, who shall here remain nameless.

Because of him, all those two billion fans from Australia to Zimbabwe almost never heard of Eaton Place.

"We were finishing the first series," John Hawkesworth told me; "I was waiting to hear whether to keep the actors signed on for a second series—when there was a big row at London Weekend and a new Controller came in."

But no word about a second series. Nor even about running this first one. "So I went to him and asked, and he said, '*Upstairs, Downstairs*? What's that?'

"After about six weeks I asked him again, and he said, 'I haven't had time to look at them . . .' and I said, 'You ought to look at *one*.'

"So he did agree to sit through one. We watched it together. In dead silence. Not a laugh. Not anything. When the tape ran out, he said, 'Well, Johnny . . . nice. Very nice.' And that was that."

But not really.

More silence. Then: "It has some nice scenes in it, Johnny, some nice filming. And that little maid—she was quite funny. It's kind of tricky. But it's very slow. And it just won't go."

Upstairs, Downstairs, it appeared, had had its first and last showing.

(From London Weekend, this footnote: The Controller went to the Director of Programmes and asked, "Do I have to put those bloody things on? I hate them!" The answer: "Yes, you have to.")

So, he went back to Hawkesworth and told him, "You're an old friend, Johnny; I'll see if I can put them on—sometime."

Not surprisingly, Hawkesworth did not press the matter of a second series. The actors were not rehired.

The Drama Controller was as good as his word. He put them on . . . at 10:15 on Sunday nights. In England, that's about as "some-time" as you can get.

"After it had run about two months (this, mind you, almost a year after we had finished it), the Controller rang me up. 'What about a second series?' " (It had received good reviews.)

" '*Crikey!*' I said. 'I don't know whether I can get the actors back!' "

And sure enough, Simon Williams (James) was appearing in a play in the West End. With a year's contract.

"Fortunately, I was able to get Freddie back." (Alfred Shaughnessy, the script editor).

"Freddie" approached the problem of James with the soft heart of a mafioso: "Can we get him back long enough to kill him off?"

They could. For one episode. And for that episode Shaughnessy wrote a story fans will never forget. But he didn't kill off James (thank goodness!); he banished him. In such ignominy, though, that Williams rather concluded he'd not be brought back.

In case you missed the episode: Sarah, now a music-hall singer, is expecting a baby by James. When the Bellamys learn of it, they pack him off to India and Sarah off to the country estate of Lady Marjorie's family, where she can have her baby out of gossip's way. Sarah leaves, alone and with touching dignity, while James—who has not uttered a word of objection—goes upstairs to pack.

The series takes on a new dimension.

And a new problem. They've thrown out the baby with the bathwater—once again, they have to think of a way to bring Sarah back. This time around, Shaughnessy has her arrive unexpectedly downstairs just as King Edward VII arrives upstairs for dinner. Her baby will arrive, roughly, with the dessert.

The show is ready to go on.

But a script editor's lot is not a happy one. He is always backstage, waiting, pen in hand, for acts of God and other uninsurable disasters. Had Shaughnessy known, when he wrote that ingenious story for clearing the decks of James, what he and everyone were soon to know, he might have kept James out of Sarah's bed. Because Pauline Collins (who played Sarah) was pregnant, and *her* baby was not due until some months *after* the dessert. So here was Sarah, having just delivered, and Pauline Collins, visibly pregnant.

Back to the drawing board for Shaughnessy. And back to bed for Sarah. But whose bed? Ah, that chauffeur—the one they were saving for Rose . . . and that is why Sarah, with such unseemly haste, goes straight from her delivery bed in the attic into Thomas' bed in the garage.

The Muse stumbled on. Dismayed, but undeterred.

7

How but in custom and in ceremony
Are innocence and beauty born?

—W. B. Yeats, "A Prayer for My Daughter"

We come now to that last and greatest commandment, the one we said deserved a chapter of its own: The characters will *speak* and *behave* as people actually spoke and behaved in such a household at such a period of time.

Well, come on now . . . since when has authenticity been allowed to stand in the way of theatrical necessities? Who cares whether Marc Antony actually spoke in those parallelisms and antitheses that Shakespeare put in his mouth? Or whether Romeos in Verona were wont to go about stabbing themselves for love?

In *Upstairs, Downstairs*, however, such cares were to govern every word, from forms of address to the substantive matters that try a writer's soul.

"The behavior was the great secret," Jeremy Paul (one of the principal writers) told me.

The simpler matters—when to say "My lady" and when "Your ladyship"—could be penciled in by Shaughnessy. As could such touches as having Hazel, who was not to the manner born, address Hudson as *Mr.* Hudson. Or the idioms—"I must go and have me lay-down," "Will her ladyship be dining in?" Or even the bygone ceremonies of civility, as when Richard, visiting Hudson's bedside after his heart attack, would not presume to sit down without first asking Hudson, "May I?"

The authenticity that could not be penciled in, and that came the hardest—going to the heart of the writer's craft—lay in the premise preceding any setting down of words—namely, that the Edwardians marched to different drummers from you and me. Imagine, for instance, the writers' consternation on being told that the upstairs people were brought up to keep their feelings to themselves, that from the nursery on they were taught to keep a stiff upper lip and were punished for any display of anger, discouraged from any display of affection—in short, they were denied all those forms of expression that are the very stuff of drama.

"It was the final challenge." Paul said. "We were always being ticked off by Freddie—'They wouldn't *say* that,' or 'No, no, no—they wouldn't *do* that.' And I would say, 'But he's angry!' And he would say, 'But that would be rude.' And I would say, 'Wouldn't he be rude?' And he would say, 'Yes, but not in that way.'

"In Edwardian England, there were rigid rules of behavior: If the roof was falling in, there were rules for handling it. John and Freddie, because of their backgrounds, understood them completely; they knew exactly how people behaved, no matter what situation they were in.

"This behavior controlled us." It determined not only the style but even the substance. "Anger, expressed, dissipates itself," Paul explained. "So, had James and Richard had a few rows all along" (instead of only the one, years earlier, when James asked Richard to move out), "there would not have been that final one. It took a long time—sixty-six episodes—before I could write that scene. It opened the wounds suppressed so long—and by then it was too late."

This formalized behavior could not be learned from the writers' research; it sprang from the memories of Hawkesworth and Shaughnessy. And that is what made *Upstairs, Downstairs* different from other historical television dramas. Research can't hold a candle to memory.

Shaughnessy grew up at 75 Eaton Place. His grandfather sat in the House of Lords; his stepfather was Equerry to the Prince of Wales, who later became Edward VIII. The Prince had come often to the house when Shaughnessy was a young boy; he "would flip over the pages of our wretched books, crammed with badly done sums, illiterate essays, and inaccurate history. All he could manage to say was 'Jolly good, you know, jolly good, you know.' For some time after, he became known to us as 'Jollygoodyeknow.' " (From Shaughnessy's biography, *Both Ends of the Candle*.)

The episode *Guest of Honor*, about an earlier Prince of Wales, was written straight from memory: the hustle, the anxiety of a household preparing for a royal guest—rehearsing the bow, dodging the tempers of edgy servants, watching from his nursery window as the policeman and onlookers gathered outside on the pavement—and, at last, seeing the red carpet rolled out.

As a young man, Shaughnessy attended house parties at many of the great country estates—Haddon Hall, Castle Howard, Leeds Castle, Sutton Place—and knew what it was like to find one's clothes laid carefully out (with the holes in the socks always—or so it seemed—turned up), one's toothpaste already squeezed onto the waiting toothbrush.

Hawkesworth, too, came from that world. "John knew it—absolutely," David Langton (Richard Bellamy) told me. "He knew the precise moment one went from a boiled shirt to a soft one. . . . Only a keen follower of the hounds could have written the hunting episode"—that harsh satire of hunting weekends and horsey talk and bridge and charades. And amorous intrigues, upstairs and down. And the downstairs gossip. "After zey come back, zey always quarrel," the French maid explains to Edward; "zen zey make love." *"Before dinner?"* he asks. "Yes, and afterwards too."

But not always with their lawful-wedded spouses.

So, both the producer and the script editor had, in a sense, been born at Number 165. Both had occupied that ambiguous space allowed to children, neither quite upstairs nor down, neither quite seen nor unseen, where they could observe the downstairs people in a way their elders upstairs never could, listening to their bickering and gossiping and imitating of their betters—not just saying "Will his lordship be requiring lunch, my lady?" And where they could observe the unending parade of rituals, rituals that would be indelibly inscribed on the tablets of their young minds.

"The way people behaved—this is what controlled our *style*," Bill Bain, one of the principal directors, recalled. "A very particular style of storytelling. Mostly about manners. Between a waltz and a polka. Each episode opened with a waltz, closed with a polka.* The waltz is civilized, elegant; the polka, gay. Everything in between should be governed by that. Nothing too raw, too harsh, too brazen." Granted, there was to be adultery, blackmail, burglary, homosexuality, manslaughter, three suicides, and a war; but the beds, the bodies, and the blood would, mostly, be kept off-camera. Even the potentially salacious stories were actually very proper—seductions in starched collars. And the big love stories were no different: James will propose to Hazel across the dinner table at the Café Royal, with the waiter at his elbow; Georgina's engagement will be sealed without so much as a chaste kiss.

"One of the things we had to learn," Bain said, "was that upper-class parents never touched their children." That was part of the pathos of the scene when Virginia Bellamy's young son, leaving his teddy bear on his bed, departs for boarding school, "to be subjected to cold showers and Latin infinitives." Though the entire household assembles to see him off, *no one* reaches out to touch him. At last, unmanned, the boy runs over and hugs his dog, then goes over to Rose and buries his face against her.

"Both John and Freddie were absolute sticklers for getting such

---

*The polka was dropped when the tone of the series deepened.

things right," Christopher Hodson, another of the directors, said. They weren't going to have 1970s feelings and actions parading through 1906 rooms.

But how were they to milk drama out of it? "By playing the style against the substance," Hodson explained, "setting up a resistance, an emotional tension."

Bain told me that a good example of this resistance, this tension, came about when he was directing the scene where James is leaving to join his regiment, on the eve of the declaration of war: Hudson, Richard, and Hazel are waiting in the entrance hall to see him off; Hudson at the door, straight and proud and solemn; Richard and Hazel side by side, like soldiers at attention. James, in his uniform, comes down the stairs, walks over to Hazel and Richard.

JAMES:	Good-bye, Father; I'll let you know where the fun is.
RICHARD:	Good-bye, old boy.
JAMES (to Hazel):	Good-bye, honey. Take care of yourself.
HAZEL:	I will. Don't worry about us.
JAMES (to Hudson):	Look after yourself; keep an eye on Father—be sure he doesn't work too hard.
HUDSON:	Good luck, sir.
JAMES:	Don't let Hudson sneak off and join up; he will, you know, if you don't watch him.

As for dialogue, nothing. As for stage business—well, James nods to Richard, kisses Hazel, shakes Hudson's hand—and he's off. One of the non-scenes of all time.

Yet, on the tape, absolutely wrenching. Why? I asked Bain. "I decided to have James and his father shake hands. It seemed a small thing to do; in my background—I'm Australian—they'd have embraced. When John came to rehearsal and saw it, he said, 'They wouldn't touch.' And I said, 'Wouldn't they?' He said, 'No, no, no, they never touched.' And it was more poignant that they stood there, looked at each other, and didn't touch. There was no release of emotion—which made you release yours. I've always thought, watching great actors, that it's not *their* ability to cry that moves you; it's their ability to make *you* cry."

How people behaved, what ceremonies made up their days—a vanished world, re-created from the memories of two men, Hawkesworth and Shaughnessy. The Marsh-Atkins story, under some other aegis and incarnation, might well have been excellent, but it would have been a different breed of cat. As told by these two men, it became a flesh-and blood history tale, so real that when the FOR SALE sign went up at Number 165 Eaton Place, we wept. For its times and its ways—for all times and all ways that have passed.

8

Where did you come from, baby dear?
Out of the everywhere into here.

—George Macdonald,
At the Back of the North Wind

To those true believers of the gospel of *Upstairs, Downstairs* as written by the media, this talk of many writers must be unsettling.

The story of Jean Marsh being the sole author got started, Hawkesworth told me, "when Jean was asked to go to the States to promote the series. It was not Jean—it was everyone else—who kept saying she had written it all. They *wanted* her to have done it. And Jean didn't deny it.

"And I didn't deny it. When people wrote me about it, infuriated, I said, 'I think it's marvellous publicity; it's going to sell the series.' I worked for J. Walter Thompson, remember. I have no ax to grind. I don't want to be a great hero. If people want to feel that she wrote all those scripts and masterminded it, why not? As long as they watch the show, let it rip!"

Everyone said much the same, up to a point—that the authorship was conferred on her by the American press, that she had never claimed it. Neither had she disclaimed it. Some laughed the whole

thing off as "Jean's bit of glory-grabbing." Others were not amused:
For their idea for a show about two servant-girls, she and Ms. Atkins
received fifty percent of all royalties; the writers, only their fee
and—it had been hoped—acknowledgment.

Hawkesworth urged me to "give Jean and Eileen all the credit
that is due; the pearl in the oyster came from them, no question."

Others I had talked with, I told him, had left me with the
impression that the original idea had been somewhat in the line of
the historically hackneyed servants' comedy—buffoonery in the scullery, spying outside the boudoir, and low-brow high jinks in the
stable. "That's the way it has always been done before; their idea
—and what made it say something entirely new and different—
was to take the servants seriously."

Were any of the characters in the series taken from the Marsh-
Atkins proposal? "Only Jean's. She contributed an enormous amount
just by producing Rose."

"And something else," he added; "she didn't interfere and she
wasn't a bore."

The Jean Marsh Myth, it might be said, is not so much untrue
as unnecessary. To have conceived *Upstairs, Downstairs* is laurel
enough—and one she needs to share with no one but Eileen Atkins.

9

In the beginning was the Word . . .
and the Word was made flesh.

—The Gospel According to St. John

But casting directors sometimes precede even the Word.

Take Mary Buck. A role custom-written for Eileen Atkins, scratched altogether when Pauline Collins was hired to replace her, and when Shaughnessy took a good hard look at Ms. Collins and created Sarah.

Remember the butler who drank his master's port and smoked his cigars and told risqué stories? He went out the window, Shaughnessy said, "when Martin Case had that inspired idea of casting Gordon Jackson for the part. Gordon is Scottish, so I changed the name to Angus, and then we made him well educated, even a little erudite—because Scots then generally were—and they were also Calvinists, slightly Puritanical, slightly rigid, so we had him saying grace and making Sarah write out the Ten Commandments."

Another of Martin's ideas was to bring in an actress of Angela Baddeley's stature to play a cook. At the very first rehearsal she transformed the role. "We abandoned the original description of the part and went along with the way Angela was playing it."

In fact, throughout the making of the series, Case insisted on bringing in top actors, even for bit parts. Like the three-line role of the waiter whom James recognizes as having been his superior officer in France—he realized that in those few lines a whole story could be implied.

And if it hadn't been for Case, we would have seen no more of James after he was banished to India, for it was at his insistence that Simon Williams was brought back to the show.

Martin Case. Whose name did not even appear in the credits. Yet both the writers and the directors thought that his casting— as much as the writing—was what made the show.

"I wanted every single one of them to be a top actor but not a star, strong enough to carry an episode on his own yet happy to be a supporting actor the next week," Case told me. "Talent to cover us *whichever way the stories went.*

"Next, I bore in mind that these people were going to be working together for a long time [the only person, at that time, with such a faith in the future of the show], so I ranked congeniality right along with talent—the way I would cast a long-running play, because temperament can ruin a cast as quickly as mediocrity. When John and I had a choice of two equally good actors, we'd go for the compatible one."

His insistence on bringing in top actors for every part seemed, to those of little faith, like sending in men to do boys' work. After all, who could have foretold, from those early outlines about Sarah and Elizabeth and James and Alfred, that the spoiled young James would become the hero? Or that he would become a symbol for all those young men of his generation who, whatever their vigor or ennui, their talents or their dilettantisms, would once and once only make a total and uncompromising commitment which, whether soon or tardily, they would pay in full? Or who could have foretold that the maid named Rose would become a symbol for the sweethearts and wives procured for spinsterhood by a Pied Piper who steals away the bridegrooms of the land? Not that Case envisioned anything so specific, but he *was* one of the few who realized from

the first that "they're on to something here—a real humdinger!"
And he was never misled into confusing "minor" with "mediocre."
Thanks to him, when the series began to strike major chords, the
actors could carry the tune.

Unlike Mrs. Bridges and Sarah and Hudson, not all the actors
created themselves out of the whirlwind. Some found themselves
slowly. "In her first few plays, Lesley-Anne Down [Georgina] was
only adequate," Hawkesworth told me. "I was in despair; Martin
and I had talked with every young actress in England, 'and now,'
I thought, 'I've chosen just a pretty face.' She was only nineteen,
with no experience except as a sex goddess in B films. It was in the
war, when she became a nurse, that talent suddenly began to
show—like a rose opening—and by the time of that scene with
James in France, she moved me to tears. From then on she never
looked back. A star. A rare thing, star quality."

Another who found himself slowly—for different reasons—was
Simon Williams, as James. "Some of us would grope along," he
said, "wondering, 'God, what am I going to do? What a disaster!'
Or sit back waiting for the writer or director to say, 'Take him that
way.' Or waiting to see how a more positive actor was playing the
thing. And the directors sometimes waiting for the actor to find
himself. And the writers watching to see what the actor made of
it. All waiting for someone to take the initiative.

"In my case I don't think I committed the character to a positive
course until quite late. I just vacillated around throughout the first
two series. I think I as an actor and the writers and producer found
the direction at the same time and we just took off. It was quite
rewarding."

His vacillation was understandable. The part he signed on for
read: ". . . weak, arrogant, young man with too much money; a
complete bounder, who thinks any kitchen maid is fair game." No
clue that he will one day fire a shot heard around the world.

Brought back to the show after that year on the stage, he didn't
know whether he was to be the prodigal son or the bad penny. "We
didn't want him to go on playing the young blood, the Guardsman-

about-town," Shaughnessy said. "We wanted the characters to develop. So John and I decided he would become a sort of loser, that nothing would go right for him—he loses his mother, whom he adores; doesn't get on well with his father; makes a miserable marriage; loses his child . . .

"When we were asked to go on through the war," Hawkesworth added, "we knew he would become an officer. We decided he would find himself, learn to feel for his men, acquire a purpose and ideals—become capable of real gallantry."

Then the postwar series. "What happened to so many young men," Hawkesworth went on, "was that the war did more than destroy them physically—it destroyed the very ideals it had implanted." So it would be with James: He would find himself, only to lose himself. Returning home, he will find things not to his liking. He will make desultory efforts to set them right; but because he has seen those things he ought not to have seen, he can believe but briefly in those endeavors by which men make sense of their lives. Even when he rallies, spasmodically, he will always find the wrong man behind the arras.

From bounder to loser to tragic symbol of an era—little wonder Williams (James) had an identity problem. He didn't even know —until I told him two years after the fact—that there had once been a plan to bring him back from the war a virtual vegetable, wheezing and drooling in a wheelchair, to be nursed into infinity by the ever-suffering Hazel.

Williams recalls that "in developing the part—imagining James' childhood, imagining his school days—I began to realize I was having trouble imagining him as an old man. I wish I'd kept a diary of my feelings toward the role, because in hindsight I wonder whether I telegraphed that to the writers." (To the contrary, Hawkesworth and Shaughnessy knew—and weren't telling.)

"At any rate, when they said to me, 'Suicide,' I knew that was perfect. Exactly right."

To add to his difficulties in finding his character, different writers were pulling him in different directions. Paul saw him as a "spoiled, self-seeking young man"; Rosemary Sisson, as a "romantic Rupert Brooke figure." Sisson was not alone; one director asked, "Can't we make him a bit more of a romantic lead?" Another, "Why does he have to be such a cad!" And the English public—he was accosted in a pub one evening as "You bloody sod."

Abuse so personal can erode the line between the actor and the character; Williams himself began to feel a loser: "I'm such a thoroughgoing rotter!" he complained to Paul.

"It's going to be all right," Paul assured him. "Who wants to plya a matinee idol? You'll get it in the end. Trust us."

"But I didn't know the end goal," Williams told me. "How did you reconcile the different characterizations of the writers?" I asked, knowing the writers were encouraged to explore characters in depth, to find complexities, surprises.

"By resisting the writing. And even by resisting James. Embracing the idea that people are complex, that whole biographies are required to describe them. Once I accepted this, I could say, 'Fine. I can be all these things all those people want, and still find another truth beneath them all—my own.' "

Resisting the writing. Resisting James. How did the writers take to this? With interest. "I'd go and watch rehearsals, to see what the actors were giving me," Paul said, "which I would then take and use. And what wasn't working, what they were not picking up, [I would stop] using."

This became one of the sources of dramatic tension in the show —everyone playing against or resisting or building on what everyone else was doing. Creatively. Not negatively. Hawkesworth and Shaughnessy. Writer and writer. Writer and actor. Actor and director.

At one point this resistance of the actors was a response to necessity—when, with new writers and new directors, an actor would have to find ways of handling inconsistencies and contradictions, or out and out balk, as Gordon Jackson did when a new director suggested Hudson sneak a drink. Later it became a deliberate technique, one that kept the series from going flat and predictable. "We would try to surprise the actor, make him think, 'I never thought that was in me,' and the actors would surprise us," Paul said, "topping it with dimensions of their own—or ignoring it altogether." The writers, too, would surprise each other: "Sometimes, watching another writer's story, I'd think, '*That's* interesting; I wouldn't have thought of that,' " Paul said; "other times, 'I can't inherit this—I don't *believe* what happened last week!' " (One surprise no one followed up on: Rose's underhanded trick of talking Daisy out of answering the ad for tram conductorettes, telling her that her loyalty was to the household . . . and then going out that very afternoon and getting the job for herself. In a script by Sisson.)

I wanted to know how, exactly, Williams went about resisting James.

"Well, sometimes a writer would give me scenes that I felt were too sweet for James, so I would do them awkwardly, trying to make it seem that even when he *wanted* to be nice, he didn't know how. Or they would give me speeches that were too fluent, too articulate for him, so I'd chop them up. Or speeches that were too long, and I'd make them sound short."

"Make a long speech sound short?" I asked.

"In that speech where he's telling the servants he is selling the house and is giving them a month's notice, I paced it as though he were going to go on *twice* as long and I try to have him thinking, in the first half, that in the second half he will speak in a more sympathetic vein; then, when he gets to that point, I act as though he is unable to go on—and he cuts it off, abruptly."

"What about the scenes where James was being so bloody awful?"

"Yes. Like that impossible scene when Georgina is in rehearsal at the movie studio," he recalled. "James at his most confused." Georgina being naive and giddy. The producer using her for her family's name. Dolly not telling her that her movie lover will be Frederick, the Bellamys' footman (doing a bit of moonlighting), and James being "volatile and pompous, throwing my weight around, embarrassing everyone, and every word I said aggravating the situation!"

"How does one save a character called on to make an ass of himself?" I asked.

"I kept having him think, under the line, 'I've no right to be here; I'm being a pompous fool, doing more harm to myself than to them.' "

It worked: Though we disliked him, we bled for him.

Another dimension, too, he brought to the scene. He made us realize that, beneath his pomposity and volatility, he was right. Not in his behavior, but in his outrage, in his conviction that something sleazy was happening. Something not limited to that studio. Maybe nothing wrong. But sleazy. And to fight it was to appear a prig.

"I tried always to remind myself," he told me, "that good acting is ambiguous."

"But isn't ambiguity often a lack of commitment to an interpretation?" I asked.

"Yes! The actor himself must be utterly without doubts. The commitment comes first—*then* the resistance. In playing James I didn't find the commitment until I decided that what James was all about was *holding in the hurt*. A child who had never been touched, except in rebuke. Reared by wet nurses, nannies, and governesses, slapped when he cried, sent from the room when he was unpleasant, then shipped off to boarding school and told to keep a stiff upper lip.

"With that kind of upbringing, James grew up emotionally inarticulate. Haunted by feelings he wasn't allowed to—and finally couldn't—express."

"This, then, was the basis of your commitment?" I asked.

"Yes. A man not too untypical of his time. The war memoirs of the officers' batmen show us men like James—a glimpse behind that facade—seeing their officers night after night writing the families of the men they'd lost, crying as they wrote. Showing feelings they never learned to show their wives or sweethearts or mothers, because tears were forbidden.

"Always searching for a few words. Even when he proposes

to Hazel. Very clever of Freddie." (Fred Shaughnessy, who wrote the episode. Never mind that to you and me James seemed fluent enough in that scene; the English, like the rich, are different from you and me.)

When it came to his relationship with Georgina, he and Lesley-Anne Down often took matters into their own hands. "The directors never agreed on our relationship; half of them hated it because we were stepcousins, and so they completely ignored the story line; the other half loved it and had us flirting even when it *wasn't* in the story line. Lesley-Anne and I resolved it by being as formal as possible in the flirty episodes—and slipping a few innuendos into those that ignored it."

This business of resisting did not always work to everyone's satisfaction. Hazel, for instance. Planned as a misfit, belonging neither upstairs nor down, knowing she couldn't quite make it past the landing, but a pleasant, funny girl who found infinite humor in the situation. Sisson, accordingly, wrote humor into the scripts she did for her. Meg Owen (who played Hazel), being a young woman of certain political principles, chose not to be amused, but to be wronged. She turned the comic lines to straight ones, the funny girl to an earnest, uptight one.

Besides finding Hazel's position in the household untenable rather than funny, she swam against the stream in other ways. Playing high scenes in a low key, for instance. When news comes that James ("Missing Presumed Killed") has been found alive, David Langton (Richard Bellamy), with the director's approval, decides just for once to let go, throw his arms up, throw his head back—only to find himself hanging out there all alone: Meg has decided to resist the scene altogether. Underacts.

Shaughnessy, who created her, was not displeased; "Meg did admittedly suggest a more still and reserved girl than we intended, and all of us later followed that line with her."

We, of course, were enchanted with the Hazel we got—painfully insecure, slightly better-than-thou, slightly priggish—but such was

Sisson's dismay that when the time came to decide who would write Hazel's death episode, the writers teased her. "Not you, Rosemary, you'd be like Charles Addams—grinning from ear to ear."

Then, Richard Bellamy. "So proper, so predictable—like a piece of furniture," Langton recalled; "of all the characters in the series, the one most likely to become a dreadful bore. Keeping him interesting, that was the challenge."

The writers were doing their bit to help—though not always pulling in the same direction, and not always coming up with the kind of help an actor wants. Paul explained: "There was Richard, this very charismatic, very acceptable character, very much in control of himself, and of the life around him—the nagging thing in the back of our minds was 'Why wasn't he a successful politician? Why wasn't he Prime Minister? What was the missing link?' Basically, of course, it was that we didn't want him to be an actual historical figure. I was always playing his weakness, and David was always pulling against the weakness. Rosemary would give him more muscle. So a lot of good-natured grumbling went on when I would write the script—'You've made me so pathetic!' he would say, and I would say, 'Well, you're not the Prime Minister, and you're not in the Cabinet; *something* is wrong with you, and I'm trying to find out what it is.' And he would say, 'I'm not Prime Minister because you've not written it into the part!' "

"It crystallizes in the end," Paul told me, "in the scene where James and Richard go at each other [the suicide episode], and James reveals Richard's failings as much as Richard reveals James'. We had latched on to an idea from that early biography that Shaughnessy wrote of him, that the weakness lay in his being The Man Who Married Lady Marjorie, in his being only a gentleman—while *she* was the daughter of an earl. He wanted to be the Liberal but had married into that great Conservative tradition and had to play the game, not because he was weak but because the system was too strong, and because he hadn't any money, and money was the great liberator. So, eventually he becomes the lodger in his own house!"

Between that limitation and Richard's natural virtues, Langton had little to sink his teeth into—none of the flighty outbursts that give an actor scope, not even a bit of lechery. But such was his handling of what they allotted him that, in the confines of the morning room, somewhere between the mantel and the chesterfield, he managed to make Richard into a symbol of that careful and informed civility which, through no failure of its own, was unable to reproduce itself.

This tandem creativity between writer and actor, like that between Hawkesworth and Shaughnessy, was workable, Williams thought, "because they trusted us; they underwrote—a kind of shorthand, a condensation—and trusted us with it." Indeed, there are scenes where the writer seems to have perfected the fine art of self-immolation—of burning all his proud words. For example: James telling Rose that all her money, which he invested for her, is lost. Big scene. Tense. Climactic. Yet, in the original script, Paul confines himself to *eight* words.

ROSE: Lost, sir?
JAMES: (nods)
ROSE: All of it gone?
JAMES: (nods)
ROSE: Nothing left?
JAMES: (nods)

(Note: Sometimes, in rehearsals, changes had to be made to accommodate that fifty-one-minute straitjacket; in this episode, when one scene had to be cut out altogether, one of the minutes saved was used to expand this scene. So the viewers saw James and Rose exchange such amenities as "Come in, Rose" and "Hudson said you wanted to talk with me, sir," heard James saying he has lost the money, saying he is sorry, assuring Rose that she'll always be taken care of in his household. But the writers, knowing they couldn't depend on getting these gifts of time, wrote in shorthand—and trusted the actors to get across the meaning and the feeling.)

Ferreting out the prime mover, as you see, can be both entertaining and enlightening. Take a simple thing, like a giggle: The deciding vote on Georgina was cast with just such a trifle. It happened the morning after the all-night treasure hunt when she and her flighty friends took the car and went to the country—and ran over and killed the farm laborer on his bicycle; Virginia (Richard's second wife) and Richard were questioning her, and she replied that she didn't honestly remember very much because she had been "squiffed on champagne." *And then she giggled.* "Who added that giggle?" I asked. "The director? Lesley-Anne herself? Or the writer?" Answer: the writer, Rosemary Anne Sisson.

The casting, like the writing, had its losers. And the merely unmemorable. All those itinerant housemaids who, unlike Sarah, were not brought back. And that last housemaid of all—Mary. Winner or loser? Opinions differ.

Mary was the new maid James encountered in the entrance hall upon his return from the States. One of those ambiguous scenes— was he flirting with her? Or just happy and friendly over being back home? She, flushing with pleasure over the attention, lingers . . . until Hudson enters and peremptorily orders her to get on with her work.

Then, in James' last hour in that house, she appears again. Why a stranger—at *this* point? He is in his room, burning his letters, sorting out his possessions. . . . "Having a tidy-up?" she asks. "Yes. Want to help?" Pleased, she moves aimlessly among his souvenirs, curious, asking questions, rambling on inconsequentially. Flirting? James, too? And if so, why *now*? She picks up the Military Cross he won at Passchendaele, tells him her uncle, too, had been at Passchendaele. Was killed there. A kind of quiet intimacy. The last bit of intimacy James is to have. And it is with a stranger. A housemaid.

Paul, who wrote the story, asked Shaughnessy whether he could bring in a new maid, because "I must have someone for James to talk to." Someone through whom the viewers could see into James' mind during his final moments in that household. Someone he *could* talk to, someone not involved in the overwrought emotions charging through Number 165. So, the new maid. Through her eyes, her remarks, her questions, we will follow James' thoughts—from the letters of Lady Marjorie and Hazel and Georgina to the war souvenirs to the picture of Hazel—to the picture of Lady Marjorie. In sum, his last look at life. His moment of tranquillity between the decision and the deed.

Surely those purposes she served well. What fault, then, did they find in her? She was to have served yet another purpose: She was to have been one of those ghosts who greeted James upon his return —along with his mother and his wife and their dead child. Sarah. And *their* dead child. Bringing James back full-circle. To all his futile devotions. Even Georgina. And to his tragic inarticulacy that made him more at ease with housemaids than with equals.

Some felt the point was made. Subtly and poignantly. Others, that it was made so subtly as not to be made at all. Some blamed the casting. "She should have looked more like Sarah," or "She didn't have Sarah's flair." Others blamed the actress. Some settled for blaming the Wig Department.

So, in one degree or another, Hudson, Mrs. Bridges, Hazel, James, and Mary Buck—Sarah—Mary—all took the Word in hand. The happy result was, as Paul Gray wrote in *Time*, a series that "gave up more vivid characters, through plotted deaths and departures, than most TV series ever introduce."

10

Why seems it so particular with thee?

—William Shakespeare, *Hamlet*

"Why did it go so much deeper into people's hearts in America?" Bain wanted to know. And Simon Williams. And others.

No one, in fact, who came over for that Boston Tea Party (the big wake on PBS) was prepared for the outpouring of feeling they encountered. "Sharing personal stories of how their families—their lives, if you will—had been affected," Bain said. "Tremendously moving. Something I shan't forget."

Why in America? And why not in Britain?

The first, obvious, and least complicated answer: *The British saw a different show.* We saw an edited show—thirteen episodes were completely removed, reducing their Series I and II to our Series I.

British Programming		American Programming	
Series I . . . Edwardiana		Series I . . . Edwardiana	
Series II . . . Edwardiana		Series II . . . . Pre-war	
Series III . . . Pre-war		Series III . . . . War	
Series IV . . . . War		Series IV . . . Postwar	
Series V . . . . Postwar			

So? you may ask.

For almost two years the British had no reason to suspect that they were watching anything more than Edwardiana, pure and simple; a top-notch period drama that would go on doing just what it was already doing so well. There was almost no clue that the series was going to move beyond this Edwardian time frame, that it was going to show an inexorably changing world, or that it was going to tell a story far larger than its parts, and different in tone and kind from its parts.

And . . . the heroes of *those* stories were not the heroes of *our* stories. Those stories were about Sarah, Elizabeth, Lady Marjorie, Thomas, Alfred, and many a forgotten under-houseparlormaid— *none of whom ever appeared in succeeding stories.*

Different time-sense, different story-sense, different heroes—and different plot emphasis: Those twenty-six stories depend heavily on situation, often sensational situations; later ones depend increasingly on character and theme. In the early ones, for example, Mrs. Bridges kidnaps a baby, an under-houseparlormaid hangs herself. . . .

And different structural techniques. Because those episodes were not attempting to tell—or shape—a larger story, they were structurally more self-contained, their techniques drawn from the theater; later ones (written after the show's future was secured), though telling stories complete in themselves, were at the same time chapters in an evolving story, and so increasingly turned to the techniques of the novel. As examples of genre dramas—romances, melodramas, drawing-room comedies—some of the early ones are little gems, treasure troves of the dramatist's tools.

A good example is Paul's "A Suitable Marriage" (about Elizabeth's German baron who turns out to be a spy and a homosexual). Richly plotted, veering toward the sensational, and stylistically a virtual sampler kit, the episode includes a story of misplaced love, a spy story, a homosexual affair, and a drawing-room comedy. The style is replete with stichomythia, dramatic irony, counterpoint conversations between three sets of characters, triple entendre, and occasional arias that sound like mock choral antiphonies. Thematically, it establishes threads that will later be developed into major strands, such as the rejection of old values by the upstairs, contrasted with the stability of the downstairs; respect as a debt due as much *to* the downstairs as *from* them; Hudson's suspiciousness of foreigners; Bellamy's dependence on his wife's money and on her family's influence; his consequent inability to be his own man in politics; and last, the irony that even his incorruptibility adds to his fetters.

The principal difference between this story and later ones is that, later, the themes (and character) often *are* the plot, and any sensationalism is no longer so much for the sake of plot as to make a statement about the times or about the moral deterioration of the upstairs.

In short, the stories of the first two series had more wit than weight, more polish than substance. They played merely on the surface of our emotions—the scope of their intent revealed in the music-hall polka that closed each episode and was later dropped, and in the ending improvised (but not used) when it looked as though history were to be aborted by the network as of 1908: a Cinderella wedding for James and Sarah. These episodes will strike minor chords, tell minor stories—with great flair and style. And with no indication whatsoever that *Upstairs, Downstairs* will in the end tell a tale about a young man who cannot assume his rightful place in Elsinore. From these light and bright and brittle beginnings the series became, unwittingly and ironically, a most appropriate vehicle for telling a twentieth-century-style tragedy in which all the heroes have shrunk to antiheroes, all the Hamlets to vain and uncommitted Prufrocks.

Here is a selective summary of these episodes —twelve of which never made it across the Atlantic.

SERIES I

Episode 3. Sarah is seduced by James—almost.
5. Elizabeth falls in love with a German baron who turns out to be (1) a spy who hopes to buy naval secrets from her father, (2) a homosexual who runs off with Alfred, the footman.
6. Lady Marjorie has an affair with a friend of James'.
7. Mary, an under-housemaid, is pregnant by the son of a former employee.
8. Emily, a kitchenmaid, hangs herself for love of a footman.
9. Mrs. Bridges kidnaps a baby.
10. Sarah, seduced by a houseguest's valet, becomes his accomplice in burglarizing the morning room.
13. Elizabeth wants to set up housekeeping with Laurence Kirbridge, a young poet; he, seeing the advantages of becoming a member of the Bellamy family, virtuously holds out for marriage.

SERIES II

Episode 1. Elizabeth's poet-husband is not the man she took him for: The physical side of love repels him.
2. Sarah is pregnant by James.
3. Elizabeth's husband provides her with a surrogate lover.
4. Elizabeth is pregnant by the surrogate lover.
6. Thomas, the chauffeur, conspires to blackmail Lady Marjorie with letters from her former lover.
11. Elizabeth, uninterested in her baby, becomes the mistress of an adventurer who, like her husband, hopes to use the Bellamys.

12. Sarah is pregnant by Thomas. (This time the Muse is not to blame—Pauline Collins, the actress, was pregnant, and showing.)

I rest my case.

The casual attitude of the British viewer becomes forgivable. What if he did miss one seduction more or less?

We, on the other hand, saw an edited version. Because of an "industrial stoppage" (strike) in England, the first six episodes of Series I had been taped in black and white. All well and good in England, but to make the show marketable in the States, LWT found that something would have to be done about those early episodes in black and white. Their solution was to rework and retape Episode 1 in color, tack on Episode 10 as Episode 2, Episode 13 as Episode 3, then mix in ten episodes from their Series II, and call the concoction Series I, American version. With the result that a number of viewers here were as baffled as Sir Geoffrey Dillon when he, having Elizabeth checked by a gynecologist to determine whether she is entitled (as she says she is) to sue for divorce on grounds of her husband's impotence, learns she is pregnant. The episode making it all clear has been dropped.

But there were advantages: We did not see Lady Marjorie in her lover's bed; we did not see endless perils of under-houseparlormaids; we did not go along for two years thinking we were watching period pieces, frozen in time; instead, we focused on the characters who were part of the main story, and, moving faster and with fewer diversionary side trips, were sooner aware of the continuum.

As the series began to tell another story, there would be other reasons, as we shall see, why we in America could take it so much to heart.

11

*You may have escaped the Titanic, but
I still have the Lusitania up my sleeve.*

—John Hawkesworth

What happened, then, that so changed the nature of the show?

One day, a day like any other, Rachel Gurney (Lady Marjorie) announced to Hawkesworth that she did not want to go on. "We were begging, on bended knees, 'Rachel, *darling*, please, *please*, don't go!" he told me. But, like Caesar, she would not be moved. And, like Caesar, she would give no reasons. "All she said was, 'I think I've done enough, really; I loved it: I love you all.' Then, when we'd worked it out—shipped her off on the *Titanic*—she said to me, 'I've made the biggest mistake of my life. Can't you find me and bring me back?' I said, 'The only person who can write a series for you now is Jacques Cousteau.' "

Another day, Nicola Pagett (Elizabeth) quit.

Still another, John Alderton (Thomas, the chauffeur).

And Pauline Collins (Sarah).

And James, remember, had departed the year before.

Upstairs, only Richard was left.

Nothing personal against Lady Marjorie, et al., but it was precisely here that the show began to find its story.

"If Lady Marjorie hadn't died, none of us would be here tonight," a writer from *The New York Times* said to Bain on the night of the Boston Tea Party (the wake on PBS). "I don't know what you mean," Bain answered. "Think about it," the writer said.

"And I have," Bain told me. "When Rachel said to John that she wasn't going on, and could not be talked out of it, I think he was in despair, because Lady Marjorie was the backbone of that house, and John couldn't for a while see his way around the fact. But when he did, when he and Freddie worked it out, I think it's what made the program take off. Because suddenly the series was plumbing more depths, getting into a different level of story. Into grief. Real grief, not just show-off grief."

With Lady Marjorie's death, we as viewers lost our innocence. Always before, the grimmer realities were tidied up—as when Sarah, so callously abandoned by James, soon forgot in Thomas' arms. If these people were now to live no longer under a special dispensation, no longer to be saved in the nick of time so that the show could go on, then our role, and our involvement, also changed. How could we go on being just amused voyeurs, peeking through Edwardian windows, if we knew that Humpty Dumpty could not, in fact, be put together again?

Real grief had come to that house and would not, like the housemaids, go away the next week.

Nor would the spirit of Lady Marjorie go away. She was the reason Hudson refused the butler's position at Somerby; she was in the shell-hole with James at Passchendaele; she was the symbol of those standards the downstairs remembered and held to; she was with James when he crossed the ocean; she was between him and Richard in their last row—and when James left his room for that rendezvous he missed at Passchendaele, her photograph would be the last thing his eyes searched out.

The tone of the series would change, but the style would not—could not. Like the household, it would *seem* the same: still elegant and literate and witty, still avoiding the harrowing—not showing us the private anguish of Richard's bereavement nor James' ordeal in the shell-hole, not bringing us to Hazel's deathbed. The modus vivendi, as before, would be to show relationships, the face one wears with the extended, omnipresent family. These people, in their bereavements, their aging, and their loneliness, would persevere with the same formality, the same restrained civility, with which they served at tea. Out of personal dignity, out of regard for others. (Just as Lady Southwold had declined to wear purple after her husband's memorial service because "it might upset the servants," Richard would worry about upsetting Hudson if he failed to dress for dinner.)

There would be a growing tension between appearance and reality. For while all would *seem* the same, nothing would *be* the same. The overt changes, as in life, would come singly—the motor car, the serving of Alexanders instead of tea—wearing at the time an innocuous face, especially in the eyes of the young. James might for a while continue to observe the forms, but with him they would become nothing more than hollow protocol, inspired no longer by a regard for others. To Georgina, Frederick, and the new maids, the forms would be meaningless, irrelevant, bordering on the contemptible.

An ever-darkening story—but told still in the diction of the drawing room.

Did Lady Marjorie have to die to bring this about? Perhaps not. But her death, coming at the same time as the departures of Elizabeth, Sarah, and Thomas, *did* give Hawkesworth and Shaughnessy a fresh start.

Coinciding with *this* fresh start was another: The *foot-dragging drama controller had been finally won over.* "Quit gobbling up history so fast!" he told them. "Make it last. Drag it out."

The show, it seemed, had secured its future but lost its actors.

In hindsight, all to the good. At the time, however, the future of the show seemed bleak indeed.

First, Shaughnessy had to find a way to kill off four incumbents all at once—while making them appear to leave singly. (For Lady Marjorie, the *Titanic*; for Elizabeth, America; for Thomas and Sarah, marriage and a motor-car shop.)

Next, Hawkesworth and Shaughnessy had to repopulate the house.

The first break: They were able to bring Simon (James) back from the West End theater.

Then the new faces: Hazel, Georgina, and Daisy. And later, Frederick and Virginia.

(And to keep us diverted while they filled the empty house, they took us to Somerby Park in the country, to hunt and shoot—and to let us watch Diane, the Huntress at the Chase. Her quarry: James.)

Hawkesworth and Shaughnessy, now assured that LWT would not cancel, could sit back and take a long look. No more extemporizing, no more last-minute scrambling around for writers, no more riding herd on those writers as they galloped off in opposite directions. (Of the next forty-two episodes, all but three would be written by Hawkesworth, Shaughnessy, Paul, and Sisson.)

"Earlier it was just another job," Paul said; "we were just feeding off John's and Freddie's stories; now we generated our own steam, shared with them the burden for coming up with ideas."

They could now get together and ask not just expedient questions such as "Who will get pregnant this time around?" but long-term questions such as the novelist asks: "What is the over-all story we are going to tell?" And "Where will it end?" They could plot their way not just through situation but through character and through history.

And history had tales to tell that parlormaids would blush to hear.

To do this, they would have to look back at those early stories and ask, "What can we find, in all those jaunty spicy tales, to build on?"

The answer: a gold mine.

Though the people had departed, they had left a world fascinating on its own terms, rich with rules and rituals. Those early cameos of an Edwardian social order, done with such unprecedented and unwavering insistence on authenticity—and done originally for their own sake—could now be put to larger uses. Could, in fact, become part of a statement. All those trifles of everyday life that had assumed the solidity and permanence of artifacts in a museum could begin to show signs of erosion.

The ceremony of Hudson serving tea, standing by itself, is just a relic; superseded by the ceremony of Frederick mixing luncheon cocktails for Georgina's friends, it tells a story. So, through the changing props and rituals, time will be made palpable. And also the shifting moral and social scene. Before a word is spoken, the blaring radio music in Mrs. Bridges' kitchen announces to us that the walls have been breached. The intrusion of disorder becomes audible. *And* visible. The telephone. The gramophone. Cigarette smoke drifting across the scene. The radio. Lipstick. Loud servants. Boisterous guests.

The recording of ceremonies and of behavior had been, from the beginning, what *Upstairs, Downstairs* was all about. Not about houseparlormaids. Or butlers. Or their masters. But about the codes and rituals by which they managed to live together. And this (along with some of the best writing and acting and directing in the business) was what made those lightweight stories say something unique; this was the point of all that insistence on authenticity; and this was the foundation on which they now would build.

Much to the marvel and disbelief of some who observed it. A team sent from the journal *Movie 21* to study the show's production was, for instance, "struck by the extraordinarily long business of Hudson laying out tea in the morning room, and all the action stopping while he did so." Didn't that worry the director? "No. That's what I wanted," Bain replied, and then asked, "Did it seem interminable?" Yes, they thought, adding, "And you seemed to do nothing to cover the time." Moreover, he had even rejected a suggestion that he could cut the time by having the tea table ready in position when Hudson enters. "I think this is partly what the scene is all about—there they all are, having this intense discussion . . . and in the middle of the bloody thing they've got to stop and bottle it up while the butler and maid come in and put tea down—who are not going to hurry, who haven't been told, 'Get in and get out fast, kids, because they're talking important business.' "

Now, with the chance to look ahead in history, Hawkesworth and Shaughnessy could ask, "What will happen to those ceremonies, to those tall narrow houses where extended families and a staff of servants moved through the rooms and through their lives in such highly orchestrated patterns of civility? What will happen to the Hudsons who guard their gates? To those codes of responsibility and service and loyalty?"

The answers they knew, of course. The highly externalized ceremonies would vanish, to be replaced by highly internalized "spontaneity"; the houses would be turned into flats and bed-sitting rooms where each lodger would live in an insular privacy where no bell tolls, where the chauffeur's quarters would become an inordinately expensive and very chic "mews house." The stories, if they were to go on that long, would be no longer about relationships in a large household and the responsibilities inherent in those relationships, but about alienation and loneliness.

They decided not to go on that far, "because the point of the whole thing," Shaughnessy said, "had been to show the relationships and lives in those old houses." They would, instead, go far enough to show the transition—the way of life, beleaguered, invaded.

Into that house—preoccupied though it had been with the comedies of the drawing room and the hopeless loves of housemaids and of Elizabeth—the world had always found its way: through Richard and his career, through Hudson and his newspaper and convictions, through Elizabeth and her suffragettes and socialists and lovers. Along with the other characters, however, that world had been expected, like everything and everyone, to "keep its place." It would now, as time and the series went on, become more and more intrusive.

Other things the writers now could do—show off all their wares, use aspects of the craft hitherto impossible: foreshadowing, reprises, recurring themes; themes that would turn from comic to sinister (Hudson's dislike of foreigners would become malevolent; his patriotism, jingoistic; his authoritarianism, fascistic . . .); themes that would turn from promising to tragic (Richard's loyalties would become his undoing . . .). By reaching into past episodes for themes, expanding and enriching them, they managed to bestow on the series a continuity that, working front-side-to into an insecure future, they had been unable to achieve before.

The growing incongruity between the style and the content, between appearance and reality, would be turned to their advantage, used to create tension and dramatic ironies. As, for example, in the reprise of the dinner for Edward VII, when the French ambassador comes for dinner: While the issue seems to be, Who will get the spoils? Who will succeed to Hudson's place? the answer is: no one. Because, while Daisy and Frederick and Edward are locked in contention, while James fusses about the wine and pours himself another whiskey, and while Georgina asks fatuous questions about the political situation, the walls are being breached.

Perhaps the most memorable dramatic irony is the Cinderella wedding, where the orphaned Georgina marries the son of a duke whose ancestral home has eighty-two bedrooms. "At least, *you'll* never have to fight a war," the blissful bride will say, as they decide to spend their lives painting, playing cricket, and growing trees. But *we* know better; we know that in nine short years she may again be nursing wounded soldiers, and that after that war, the dukes with eighty-two bedrooms would live in a small corner of their great houses, would resort to offering tourists a snobbish form of bed-and-breakfast: Dinner with a Duke—£50.

(Little wonder we cried at the wedding.)

A few of the reprises you may remember: Twice James, returning home from abroad, will look at the new under-houseparlormaid and be reminded of Sarah and the child she lost—once, returning from India; again, from America. And Virginia's young son will leave for boarding school in a farewell scene reminiscent of that stiff-upper-lipped scene when James left for war. And those ghosts who turn up at the servants' entrance—Alfred, fleeing the police; Sarah, in labor; Miss Roberts (Lady Marjorie's personal maid), rescued from the *Titanic*.

This repeated and careful attention to reprises, one cannot help feeling, was akin to whatever might impel a writer to write down his best sonnet in vanishing ink. What wan hope did they harbor, in a medium with week-long intermissions and nine months' "summer" breaks, that the viewers' memories would encompass such niceties? Four years after the fact, how many of us noticed the contrasts between the two dinner parties? Or remembered all that much about James' affair with a maid named Sarah who had had—and lost—a baby? Or realized the significance of James' remark to Hudson after his crossing from America, "I don't care for the ocean much"? And there were no reviewers out there remembering—and reminding us—of these merits.

Now, being forced into a fresh start by the mass exodus of actors, and being assured of future contracts, the writers could choose (and Hawkesworth could put under contract) the principal figures through whom their story would be told, the central figure around whom it would be built (James), and where it would end.

Once those decisions had been made, history took them by the hand. James' story and England's became one and the same—James would survive the war, but he would never again thrive at anything he touched.

Step by step, like the novelist, they began to plot each character's way.

Even Edward, the footman's. In the early series, just a cheeky guy, a bit of a comic, now the writers could draw him in depth. He would become a symbol of the historical unrest of the working classes, of the little man who thinks for himself—whether the answers are coming from Hudson or the dock workers. Above all, a symbol of the sheer decency occasionally found in such men, for Edward would never become one of those who use justice as a banner to front for their personal viciousness. Growing still older, he would become the archetypal complacent husband, prodded by the pushy wife.

Daisy. The archetypal scold. That she never became more has to do, I think, with the limitations of the actress. Sir Geoffrey Dillon could have sooner wrung a tear from me than Daisy.

Rose. She would blossom, briefly, into womanhood. Escaping the womb, at last. Panicking, again, back to Number 165. Then, the same war that would give her and Gregory a second chance would make her one of those thousands of England's war spinsters who would grow old enjoying other women's weddings, other women's children.

Mrs. Bridges would not change—nor Sir Geoffrey Dillon. For different reasons. Mrs. Bridges, because she was our emotional valve, releasing the tension. Dillon, because the clear-eyed pragmatists never have a core of their own; hence, they never need to make the adaptations that sear the souls of other men.

One of the new characters is Georgina, the orphaned cousin who arrives at Eaton Place with her teddy bear and grows into the young woman in a romantic white dress who will run laughing across the green lawns of a country estate on the eve of war; then into that saddened nurse standing with James in a field of war graves; on into the flapper standing over the dead body of the farm laborer she has run down in Richard's car; to end as the happy bride.

And James' journey could not only be plotted ahead, but foreshadowed: Lying in a shell-hole at Passchendaele, James sees a German staff officer "working his way through the trees . . . killing off our wounded with his revolver. Coming towards me, nearer. I tried to get my own revolver out of its holster, but I had no strength in my fingers. He saw me. He was standing just a few paces away; it was him or me. He raised his pistol, took careful aim, and I was fumbling with the damned trigger. I was done for. We stared at each other, and then, inexplicably, he dropped his arm. He stood there, watching me while I finally got a grip on the trigger and fired. I blew the top of his head off. Why didn't he kill me? I can only think he was killing the worst of our wounded, humanely, to spare them suffering. And he saw me and I didn't look so bad. Is that why? I felt we were brothers—or even the same person—and it didn't matter who killed who. It wasn't important. And what happens now isn't important. It has no meaning."

"Why didn't he kill me?" An enigma that would haunt James right down to the writing of the suicide note.

Though James didn't know it, his wounds at Passchendaele *were* fatal. Not sudden, but a slow hemorrhaging. He would be eleven years in dying. Bringing him through those years, that was to be the next challenge for the writers. "When you see the series the second time," Simon said, "you can see each letting of blood; you think, 'He doesn't know it yet, but this moment is taking him yards closer; this moment is going to come back and hit him. . . .' " All those failures and losses—he fails in the bi-election; fails in his marriage; he loses Georgina; loses his money; fails his best friend by having an affair with his wife; fails Rose by losing her savings. "And the crowning thing that goads him beyond all that was his father telling him he has failed his mother, that 'she would have been appalled.' When people ask me why I—James, that is—committed suicide, I say, 'If you have to ask, you can't have been watching very closely.' "

Through James and Georgina we will see what happens to the standards Hudson and Lady Marjorie and Richard upheld. Like so many heirs of privilege, they will view the fruits of these standards—and traditions—as something bought and paid for, rather than as something earned, as Richard had earned them—with an abiding sense of responsibility toward those who served him. Responsibility—the ever-recurring theme. So long as that responsibility goes both ways, upstairs and down, the center will hold. When the upstairs reneges on the compact, the culture falters and fails.

Richard, the writers decided, was not to be an evolving character like James and Georgina. Instead, it would be his life and his times that would change, showing him in different lights, while he himself would remain perfectly static—and solid. We had grown to know him in his prime—influential in the government, financially well off (though dependent), surrounded by his family, harassed by continual domestic crises upstairs and down, but always resilient. "The natural gentleman, not the gentleman by fiat, not the blue blood," David Langton, the actor who played him, recalled. Educated, rational, mannerly, decent, dignified, tolerant. Never impulsive, frivolous, belligerent, avaricious, or vengeful. Possessed, in short, of all those gifts civilization can bestow on a man. Now we were to know him buffeted by tragedy, increasingly alone, occupying Number 165 on his son's sufferance, watching his influence wane and his world disintegrate; but he himself would remain constant, as true in adversity to the values by which he lived as he had been in more providential times. He would, as the show goes on, become a symbol of that final flowering of a culture which, inexplicably, carries a blighted seed; for such men it becomes their unnatural lot to bear sons who cannot, or will not, lay hold upon their legacies, sons who watch, idle, dismayed, indifferent—or hostile—as the world of their fathers disappears from the earth.

Interestingly, Richard and James would have but one quality in common: forbearance and compassion in the face of their wives' infidelity. James may make an unholy scene when Hazel goes down to the kitchen to help Ruby, but when he discovers the love letters from her pilot, he asks her to join him in a walk.

And Hudson. Fans' dinner parties have broken into dissension over Hudson, some guests contending he was a pious Goody Two-shoes; others, a dastardly fascist; still others, the pillar of the house. True, the Bible-quoting, foreigner-hating, superpatriotic Hudson did offer "many simplistic ruts for us as writers to fall into—some comical, some sinister—the snob, the religious maniac, the paranoid authoritarian," Sisson recalled, "but we always pulled back, found other qualities."

Hudson would become not the stock figure of ridicule, not the anathema of authority outdoing itself, but the pathetic, rigid man who lives to see his very virtues become fit fodder for reformers.

Going into the war, the writers will reveal the dark potential in such a man, a man who, pushed to the edge, could have become either a tragic hero or a tragic villain; he has the strength of mind and will that impels such figures to the brink, but he lacks the single-mindedness: Tragic heroes and villains are not deterred by personal loyalties; Hudson is. In the pinch Hudson's greatest loyalty is not to his convictions or to his prejudices—but to people. Because of his convictions he resigns his position at Number 165—when James *orders* him to serve Richard's best claret at lunch with Miss Forrest; because of his loyalty he will withdraw the resignation— he cannot upset Lady Marjorie or her house on the eve of her departure for America.

Again, soon after Lady Marjorie's death, amid speculation about closing Number 165, Hudson is offered the post of butler at Somerby Park, one of England's vast and storied country estates. Though the stone-faced Hudson gives us no clue as to why he tears up his letter of acceptance, the camera does—it shows his eyes falling on a picture of Lady Marjorie. The retiring butler at Somerby puts it into words for us: "It's a big responsibility, this place; I didn't mind it so much when his old lordship was alive, but now when it comes to maintaining standards, it's all on *my* shoulders. I sometimes think that going into service is like getting married: You live in the same house, you back each other up, you quarrel sometimes, but you make your life together. But when the master dies" (we hear Hudson in a quiet counterpoint, adding, "Or the mistress") "you are expected to carry on just as if nothing happened, but you can't. It's a question of loyalty, you see." (Hudson adding softly, "Yes.") "Yes—a question of loyalty."

As time and the series go on, Hudson and Richard will be given many qualities in common. Both live by objective standards—and have little stomach for those who live by personal ones. Both are always in control of themselves. Both are well-informed. Deliberate.

Dependable—whatever happens, from housemaids in childbirth to spies in the boudoir to missing-presumed-killed telegrams from the War Office, Hudson and Richard face up to the responsibility of authority. *They cope.* Unlike James, unlike modern father figures, who often refuse to become involved.

And a sadder similarity—both men personify a dying culture: Richard, as one who profits from it; Hudson, as one who does not but who will uphold it even when those who do so profit will not go to the trouble.

But Hudson is something more: He is the guardian of the gates. And as such it will become his tragic lot to let in at the door, against his will, all the forces that will destroy the house.

So, when Lady Marjorie and Elizabeth and Sarah and Thomas—not to mention other assorted housemaids who had come and gone—abandoned the ship, and when the Drama Controller came aboard, so to speak, the series headed for deeper waters.

Though the camera would still be focused on the morning room and servants' hall, it would show a household wearing mourning bands, Hazel hanging blackout curtains and not living to take them down, Hudson putting fewer coals on the fire; and little by little we would notice that, though the mourning bands were long since discarded, the blackout curtains removed, pools of darkness had collected in the teacups.

12

A wandering minstrel I—
A thing of shreds and patches.

—W. S. Gilbert, *The Mikado*

"We call them the Gussets," Hawkesworth said. "They don't fit properly."

The Gussets were three added episodes, taped after the series was completely finished.

"*After* James' suicide?" I asked.

"Yes. After the moving men had already carried off the chester-field from the morning room."

London Weekend had been pushing for them to go on another year, and they had been saying, "No, we've told our story—about twelve people living under one roof in a mutually supportive relationship—that story had to come to an end."

London Weekend suggested a compromise—three more episodes.

Now? With James in his grave and the house empty?

"Intersperse them."

At last, they agreed. But Shaughnessy got very gray—sorting the threads of the plots, making space among the developing themes, trying not to interrupt the carefully accelerating momentum of that inexorable journey to Maidenhead.

The three new stories were then interspersed after Episodes 9, 10, and 11. No one was completely happy with the outcome—except the viewers. And James, who got resurrected from the grave.

But who can quarrel with an expediency that brought us Hudson's heart attack, the holiday in Scotland, and Ruby's job as the cook-general in the snobbish middle-class household?

A look at these "fillers" tells almost all we need to know about the quality of effort that went into the writing.

"Will Ye No' Come Back Again?" (Sisson) takes Richard, James, Georgina, Hudson, Mrs. Bridges, and Ruby to Scotland, where, with no one to impress, they still dress for dinner; where, because their wine is late in arriving, they are reduced to the shocking experiment of drinking whiskey before dinner; where James and Georgina have their last happy moments together before the ghost of their old love walks in; where James, rejected, decides to leave for America (tricky, because they had already taped that other final rejection, before the suicide); where Hudson takes his last look back at the land of his youth and where we are given the feeling through-out that all of them, for a long while now, have been visiting in a land to which they can "no come back again." (None of all this, by the way, had anything to do with the main plot: Hudson's unmasking of the salmon poacher. Which in turn had nothing to do with the main story of the series—which, after all, had already been told and taped. . . .)

"Noblesse Oblige" (Hawkesworth), sandwiched in just before the suicide episode, tries to keep the continuity going—while actually stopping it—by inserting the story of the enforced separation of Georgina and her fiancé. Its real interest is in the variations it plays on its title: in Mrs. Bridges' tyrannical badgering of the dim-witted Ruby; in Georgina's and Robert's complacency in planning a married life filled with "painting, cricket, and forestry" (but "no politics"); in the fiancé's mother, whose coldness is veneered with exquisite politeness; in Ruby's pretentious, middle-class employer, who coddles her lapdog and exploits her maid; in Mrs. Bridges' spiteful reluctance to give Ruby a reference versus Richard's magnanimity, although (lovely touch!) when he sits down to write it, he doesn't know Ruby's last name. Still and all, that obligations are the essence of noblesse oblige *no one but Richard remembers*.

While Hawkesworth is playing these variations on the theme, he is also bringing the changing world through the doors of Eaton Place—in the person of Ruby's replacement, Mabel Wilks. The wages and hours Mabel demands (38 pounds a year and a day off a week) are beyond anything Number 165 has ever heard of. "Blackmail!" declares Georgina, who is going to live in the house with eighty-two bedrooms. As for Mabel, the concepts of service, responsibility, loyalty, or standards are beyond anything *she* has ever heard of. She *has* heard of equality, which she seems to interpret as the right to lip off and goof off. She will play the kitchen radio full-blast, she will smoke when she feels like it, dance when she feels like it, sing when she feels like it—and she feels like it in the middle of the working day. Mrs. Bridges, hearing her, storms into the kitchen with "Stop that caterwauling this instant! I won't have no singin' in my kitchen!"

Well, the downstairs had, in its time, seen plenty of "cheek"— remember Sarah? Criminality, even—Alfred holding Edward hostage at knife-point, Thomas blackmailing Lady Marjorie and Richard —simultaneously. And endured them all. Mere verminous villainies. This new kitchenmaid was a new—and graver—threat: When told by Mrs. Bridges to "wash them pans again," the girl looks her in the eye—and gives her the raspberry, then starts toward the door for her afternoon off.

Oh, what a falling off was here!

As for Mrs. Bridges, she is too apoplectic to give the girl what-for.

It gets delivered by Daisy, the resident rebel (old-style, that is), who gives the girl a smart slap in the face.

Cheered on by that other old-style rebel, Edward: "Good girl, Daze!"

Like Mrs. Bridges, they too are suddenly out of date.

And then, "The Understudy" (Paul) shows why an American producer said he could have milked five stories out of any one of theirs. Its themes: loyalty, responsibility (from political to domestic), the demands of excellence, the deterioration of order, the standards of Lady Marjorie and Hudson, the stigma of Edward's war record, the fear of old age, the fear of abandonment, the affection between Hudson and Mrs. Bridges. . . . The episode is a reprise of Shaughnessy's very early one about Edward VII coming to dinner —but with sad differences that tell a story in themselves. This time the occasion is a dinner for the French ambassador; France and England are in serious disagreement about allowing Germany into the League of Nations; the relevance of the Treaty of Locarno is in question—so to Richard, informed and involved, the dinner is of international importance; to James and Georgina, uninformed and uninterested, it is merely an intrusion into their polo and sailing, an intrusion they nevertheless consent to, out of a sense of family loyalty and responsibility.

James' concern is reserved for the menu, the wine, and the protocol. He says to Richard, "The wine's the important thing;" to Georgina, "With the port going round, you turn to Lady ——." These are the things he knows—and bothers about. And he doesn't even know these very well—Richard bests him on the wine, and Mrs. Bridges on the menu. A whole story in a few moments: What happens to a culture when its young elite cares more for form than for substance, when ceremonies have degenerated into protocol?

The downstairs plot is a dual one—about Hudson's heart attack on the night of the party and about the dogs of ambition and greed at once let loose. Who will announce the guests? Be in charge of the wine? In short, succeed Hudson? A war of succession breaks out. Though purportedly between Frederick and Edward, it is Daisy who starts it and who keeps it going—goading Frederick until he has no choice but to return the fire, taunting Edward for letting her fight his fight, tattling to Georgina, implying that Frederick's studying and initiative—indeed, his very excellence—are suspect, subversive. Frederick, other than rising to a bit of sarcasm, remains, as always, cool and inscrutable—even magnanimous, helping Edward with the ambassador's name, reminding him to decant the claret. Edward throughout is passive, apprehensive—and decent, embarrassed by Daisy's viciousness.

While the battle rages, the hour for the dinner party approaches. Hudson is in his bed, barely conscious. Mrs. Bridges is devastated with grief. Who will save the day? The old guard—Rose and Richard. Upstairs, Richard makes the necessary decisions, instills confidence in the panicking Edward, sends his good wishes to Mrs. Bridges, encourages a nervous Georgina—while James pours a drink for himself and for Georgina and fusses on about the wine. Downstairs, Rose gets Mrs. Bridges to a chair, soothes her, gives her brandy, and steadies Ruby for the job of taking over the cooking. (She will deal with the vultures . . . but later.)

And when she does (as they start going at it again), she turns on them with both fury and contempt:

ROSE: You give me the pip, you do. There's poor Mr. Hudson lyin' there fightin' for his life and you got him buried already!
FREDERICK: Only bein' practical. House has got to go on functionin'.
ROSE: Not with you in charge it hasn't. Neither of you. The way you're carryin' on—behavin' like jackals. You disgust me, the lot of you.

Richard, Hudson, Mrs. Bridges, and Rose—the only ones who, throughout the crisis, think primarily of others. Though the house belongs to James, though the servants are James' responsibility, Richard is the one who makes the arrangements for Hudson's convalescence, assures him the post of butler will be his as long as he wants it, arranges for an ambulance to take him to the country, and ad infinitum. Hudson, ill as he is, focuses his concern on the running

of the household and on Mrs. Bridges; his last words, spoken to
Rose on being wheeled out to the ambulance, are "Take care of Mrs.
Bridges for me, will you?"

First, Lady Marjorie. Now Hudson. Someday, Richard. We know
the center cannot hold much longer.

But for now, there remains a moment of staying, an epiphany,
when all that is past remains intact, suspended outside of time and
gravity, a moment during Richard's visit at Hudson's bedside—
after he has *asked permission* to sit down, after he has explained the
arrangements for the convalescence, given assurances about the doc-
tor's report and about the post of butler being his "as long as he
wants it"—when Richard asks:

RICHARD: What's that you're reading?

HUDSON: Oh . . . I've taken to reading some poetry, my lord.

RICHARD: Robert Burns?

HUDSON: Alfred, Lord Tennyson, my lord. Rose found it on my
shelves. I didn't know I possessed it.

RICHARD: *Idylls of the King?*

HUDSON: *The Lady of Shalott* is my particular favorite, my lord.

RICHARD: *The Lady of Shalott.* I learnt that at school. Wonder if I
can remember any of it. (He starts to quote at random.)
"On either side the river lie
Long fields of barley and of rye . . ."
(Richard searches for the line.)

HUDSON: If I may . . .

RICHARD: Yes?

HUDSON: "That clothe the wold and meet the sky;"

RICHARD: "And thro' the field the road runs by . . ."

HUDSON: "To many-tower'd Camelot; . . ."

RICHARD: "Willows whiten, aspens quiver, . . ."

HUDSON: "Little breezes dusk and shiver
Thro' the wave that runs for ever
By the island in the river. . . ."

RICHARD: Yes. "Only reapers, reaping early
                In among the bearded barley . . ."
HUDSON: " 'Tirra lirra,' by the river
             Sang Sir Lancelot."

Lancelot . . . Camelot.

13

What's Hecuba to him, or he to
Hecuba,
That he should weep for her?

—William Shakespeare, *Hamlet*

Camelot. The Garden of Eden. The New World. The Old West.

Those lands of lost promise. And the stories we tell ourselves about them—the lands where we betrayed our own hopes. Such stories all peoples in all ages have told themselves—it is how we explain our human condition.

These stories—distanced from us always in space and time and ways—tend to take on the forms of legends and of myth.

Perhaps in this very distancing lies the answer to the question Bill Bain and the others kept asking, "Why did it go so much deeper into American hearts?"

To the British, *Upstairs, Downstairs* was no myth. It was history. Family history, even. For on many a British mantelpiece rests a picture of a young man like James, in his war uniform, a young man who didn't come back, or who came back, like James, too shattered in body or soul to restore his country to its vigor. Nothing mythic, nothing romantic about it. Just painfully real.

Equally real to the British were all those ceremonies and civilities of life at Eaton Place. Gone, of course. Like their silver tea sets, which can be seen in secondhand stores, where American tourists buy them and bring them home as talismans of that way of life.

Transplanted across the ocean, where mantelpieces are not altars to dead heroes, where the ceremonies of 165 Eaton Place are as romantically distant as the tournaments and banquets of King Arthur's Court, the story could take on a mythic truth, the sort of truth that makes it safe for us to weep. For it is always safer to weep for Hecuba or Lancelot than for ourselves.

And let it be remembered that *Camelot*, in the late sixties and early seventies, was one of our most popular musicals and movies. James, though, is even more our cup of tea than Lancelot. Born, like us, to an impeccable address, he finds, like us, infinite fault with the arrangements, intends to better them, suffers ennui, and meanwhile takes his best friend's wife to bed. Here was just the hero we could understand, who even had the sort of king we could find believable—a king who didn't lead armies or make stirring speeches, or do much of anything but enjoy the women and play bridge and blow cigar smoke in his partner's face.

Not least, the form the story took was just such a form as could speak to us—a sad tale told in a sprightly way, a comedy of manners, with a melodrama here and there, a few love stories, and a few laughs. Ending (if we didn't look too closely) with a Cinderella wedding.

One could even choose not to weep at all.

14

*I know that's a secret, for it's
whispered everywhere.*

—William Congreve, *Love for Love*

"Along toward the end," Shaughnessy told me, "we
were besieged by reporters, all asking the same question: 'How do
you account for the show's success? What's the secret?' "

When told, "The behavior," they were uninterested. Because
what they were looking for was a key that could be copied and used
again.

Actually, other keys were lying around, free for the having, but
only a few got copied.

Think of it: Here was a show with the budget of a sitcom or a
soap opera, getting along year after year with the same old sets,
without action sequences, without special effects, without music,
with nothing but talk-talk-talk. . . .

And it became the most popular show ever made—shown in
seventy countries, dubbed into more than a dozen languages, with
an estimated one billion viewers.

Unforgivable.

To make matters worse, it was also acclaimed by the critics. By the intelligentsia, no less!

So there *was* a public out there with taste. And here, at last, was our vindication—after all those years of being told that all the mindless razzle-dazzle served to us over the airwaves was exactly what we deserved.

In *Upstairs, Downstairs* we had been served nothing but words, well written, well acted, and well directed—and we had loved it.

That key to the show's success the television industry did not choose to copy.

Though they did copy others: the use of muted colors; the idea of bringing in a fine actor for a single episode; the notion of letting characters develop, change, before our eyes; they even tried letting the years go by in other series that were not based on novels and history.

But even as *Upstairs, Downstairs* was being made, its medium—tape—was going out of style. By the time the series ended, television drama was wedded to film. And the offspring of film is as different from that of the old ways of taping as cinema from legitimate theater.

The tape, unable to move about, was verbal. Film is visual. The tape depended on the writers and actors; film, on the technicians. The scripts for *Upstairs, Downstairs* can be *read*. Like stage plays, they tell their stories in dialogue. Try to imagine *reading* a script of *Miami Vice*. Or even Ingmar Bergman.

If *Upstairs, Downstairs* were to be made today, it would, no doubt, be made on film. And would, no doubt, be wonderful. But it might well be more of a historical saga and less of a drama.

We might well follow Richard to the House of Lords, Hudson on his rounds as air-raid warden, James to his polo matches and to the trenches in France; we might see the crowds at Buckingham Palace keeping the vigil as the king lay dying, might join the crowds on the eve of war—surging through the streets, chanting, "We want war! We want war!"

But as the writers were limited to those fixed cameras and those few sets at 165 Eaton Place, we listened to Richard in the morning room *telling* about the debates in the House of Lords; we listened to Georgina *telling* about her balls; we listened, through the windows of Eaton Place, to the shouting and singing of the crowds in the street awaiting the announcement that England was at war.

So, due to the limitations of the medium, what we watched were not vast visual swatches of history but personal stories. Dramas; not epic, not saga. Not the great events of history, per se, but how those events intruded themselves into the morning room, the servants' hall, and what they meant in the lives of a debutante, a housemaid, a man-about-town, a footman, a member of the House of Lords, and how these people lived together in supportive relationships—and with civility.

Yet in telling these personal stories the history got told as it had never been told before—so well, in fact, that *Upstairs, Downstairs* has ever since been used in English schools in history classes. (A great satisfaction to Hawkesworth, who is himself a historian.)

Another glaring but uncopied key to the series: It was not based on Henry James or Evelyn Waugh or Thomas Hardy or Charles Dickens or Honoré de Balzac or Gustave Flaubert—or on jazzed-up biographies. Hawkesworth and Shaughnessy told *not someone else's story but their own, a story never told before,* in a manner never tried before, about a way of life they once knew and what happened to it.

Just as all great stories get told.

No secret about it.

A new order—1912.

Richard and Miss Forrest. (Episode 1, "Miss Forrest.")

A hunting party at Somerby. (Episode 8, "The Bolter.")

James, dressed to ride to hounds. (Episode 8, "The Bolter.")

Two new faces at Eaton Place. (Episode 9, "Good Will to All Men.")

Rose meets an Australian sheep farmer. (Episode 11, "The Perfect Stranger.")

Hazel forgets her place. (Episode 12, "Distant Thunder.")

"After the ball is over . . ." (Episode 12, "Distant Thunder.")

A holiday at the seaside. (Episode 13, "The Sudden Storm.")

Bathing belles. (Episode 13, "The Sudden Storm.")

"I refuse to drink a toast to war." (Episode 13, "The Sudden Storm.")

PART 2

The Skeletons in
Hudson's Pantry

For those who, when the series ended, cried,
"More! Send us more!"

1

*Why, sometimes I've believed as many
as six impossible things before
breakfast.*

—Lewis Carroll, *Through the Looking-Glass*

Remember Thomas, the chauffeur, who blackmailed the Bellamys, reminding them of the family secrets he knew?

Well, now that the moving van has pulled away with the chesterfield from the morning room, we can tell a few secrets of our own . . . about his affair with Rose, for instance. And with Elizabeth.

And about Hudson's illegitimate child.

And about Richard and Hazel!

What happened to these stories? Were they shredded? Deep-sixed?

Some of them. Most of them, though, were transformed, the way the series itself was transformed, from housemaid's lark to a story of an era. Rose's affair will become a game of blindman's buff, Hudson's illegitimate child . . .

To watch the transformation is to be afforded an early-morning glimpse of the Muse, before her hair is combed; here she is, sleepy-eyed, sowing daffodil fluff among the petunias, dreamily confident a giant oak will grow.

These untold tales have never before been written down, except in Shaughnessy's notebooks, and have never been shared, except with Hawkesworth. Some of them died aborning. And we can see why. Some—even of those that got as far as fully developed story lines—were tossed away in favor of later ideas. The most interesting, perhaps, are those that grow from ugly ducklings into swans.

"Remember," Paul cautioned me, "a script editor's story lines read badly. Because they're just headlines, like 'James is drunk.' But these headlines are part of the process, the excess, before one reaches the subtle, informed middle area."

Here they are then—the roads untaken on the journey to Maidenhead. The apocrypha of *Upstairs, Downstairs*.

2

He thought he saw an Elephant
That practised on a fife:
He looked again, and found it was
A letter from his wife.

—Lewis Carroll, *Sylvie and Bruno*

SERIES I

1. "The butler gets the sack for selling political secrets to the press."* (The Hudson we knew was not waiting, full-grown, to pop out of a writer's head; he was born in the labor of false starts.)

2. Rose almost sets off the guns of war. Not just because she spills the trifle in the German ambassador's lap (for that she gets fired), but because she refuses to grant sexual favors to the young counselor sent around from the German Embassy to intervene in her behalf. "So Rose is faced with keeping her trap shut or precipitating World War I by a year or two." All for a spilled trifle.

*The passages in quotation marks are taken verbatim from Shaughnessy's notes.

3. Plan Number 1 for Richard's downfall (inspired by the Marconi share scandal involving Lloyd George): He has been relaying privileged information, obtained through his post in the Ministry of Defense, to the managing director of an armaments manufacturer and, on the strength of this, has been making a fortune in armaments stocks. The papers get hold of it, and between the press *and the servants,* he is pilloried before he can even plead in his own defense.

This trite plot, completely reworked, would later reappear in Series III—no longer a melodrama of corruption and comeuppance, but a tapestry of some of the central themes of the series: loyalty, financial dependence, women's values versus men's values, and aristocratic standards versus middle-class standards. In the reworked version the information is relayed the other way around—a friend at Richard's club, learning he is living as a boarder at his son's house, wants to help:

CHATHAM: Do you ever gamble on the stock market?
RICHARD: Never. All a mystery to me.
(Chatham seems to change his mind, says he has to catch his train, says good-bye, puts on his hat and coat, goes to the door—then turns back. . . .)
CHATHAM: I'd like to give you a tip, if I may.
RICHARD: Well, thank you, but I never back horses.
CHATHAM: No, it isn't a horse. Any spare cash you do have, anything you can raise, buy Cartwright's Engineering, a motor-car firm—it might just ease your situation.
RICHARD: That's very kind of you, but surely all motor-car firms are as dead as dodos—too much competition for too little market. . . .
CHATHAM: You *will* be sorry if you don't. . . .
RICHARD: You mean that?
CHATHAM: But there is one thing you must promise me—for rea-

sons I cannot disclose—you must not mention to anyone
that I told you to buy them. It must be absolutely
confidential.

RICHARD: Word of honor . . .

Richard buys, the stock soars; the press, learning that the company has received a defense contract and that a member of the
government has invested in it, raises questions about his misuse of
privileged information, and Richard becomes the subject of a House
investigation that threatens to wreck his career, bring down his
party, and bring disgrace on his family (not to speak of Mrs. Bridges
carrying on as though she's been personally violated).

To save the situation, Richard needs only to divulge the source
of his information, but, to Sir Geoffrey Dillon's disgust and Hazel's
dismay, he adamantly refuses. So, undertaking some sleuthing on
her own, Hazel discovers—and discloses—the man's identity, and
Richard is exonerated. But outraged.

RICHARD: How dare you? Going to my club . . .

HAZEL: I didn't go to your club.

RICHARD: Sending my servant . . . involving a servant in my affairs . . .

HAZEL: Someone had to . . .

RICHARD: Clubs exist so that women and servants can't meddle.

HAZEL: Then you are a fool. Do you think I give a damn about
your word-of-honor, hand-on-the-heart, public-school
code?

RICHARD: Such things matter to a man.

HAZEL: They don't matter to a woman—any woman. We fight
for things that do matter, like our families. And you are
my family—like it or not.

RICHARD: Women should keep out of men's affairs.

HAZEL: Keep out! Newspapers, servants leaving, and those that
are here, in turmoil . . .

RICHARD: I don't care—it was wrong of you and Sir Geoffrey to force Chatham's name out into the open against his will. It will possibly get him into serious trouble with his company.

HAZEL: He should have come forward, but he didn't dare! The man's a coward. (Softening, pleading.) Oh, Richard, please, don't be angry, just because you needed help.

RICHARD: I am angry because you behaved willfully and improperly. Clearly, your ways are not yet our ways.

HAZEL: (sarcastically) I am sorry about that. I frequently think that you and James are insane.

RICHARD: Because we have standards?

HAZEL: I have standards and I obey them. You won't convince me I've done anything wrong.

RICHARD: Our ways will have to become your ways. About that there can be no argument. I suggest you start working on it this very minute. (Walking to study door, opening it for her.) Now—please leave my study.

THE END

4. Richard, returning unexpectedly from the country, finds James in bed with a girl from the music hall. (Even in this light-weight story the crucial theme was to have been loyalty, for what triggers Richard's outrage is that James, in using Rose to cover up for him, has presented her with a conflict of loyalties.)

5. The chauffeur delivers a bombshell downstairs: He has found out that Richard's mistress is German. The servants are agog. "Most likely a spy! And what with the master in the Ministry!"

6. Plan Number 2 for Richard's downfall: Richard brings home, from his constituency in Battersea, a ragged and starving fifteen-year-old girl. Again, the servants build a worst-case

theory—i.e., dirty old man. They talk, the story gets to his political enemies, there is a scandal. . . . (The downstairs, it will be noted, is not at this stage outstanding for its compassion or tolerance—or discretion.)

The story that developed from this was the one about the pregnant housemaid whom Bellamy tries to help, only to find himself suspected of being the father.

7. Plan Number 3 for Richard's downfall: Rose and Sarah become "unwittingly involved in a conspiracy which becomes a major scandal and threatens Mr. Bellamy's chances of becoming Prime Minister."

In Plan Number 1, Richard was little more than a rich miscreant, getting what he deserved; in Numbers 2 and 3 he was a mere victim, a figure of pathos and of melodrama. In the final plans, however, there is nothing so neat nor so dramatic nor so nameable as a "downfall." Rather, Richard will miss his chance for greatness and know—too late—where and how. It will have come about not through the chicanery of others, but through his own character and the ineluctable thread of history. This more tragic story had been a part of Shaughnessy's thinking from the beginning; even before the casting, in his "Biography of Richard Bellamy," he had written, "On the surface a Tory, and married into a big Tory family, Bellamy (with his fairly humble background in a parsonage) nurses lurking but suppressed feelings for the Liberal cause. But he dare not declare this . . . his tragedy will be that he misses high office and power, when the Liberals sweep the board in 1906, through being, for reasons of patronage and his marriage, on the wrong side of the House."

Though these more melodramatic ideas would later present themselves to Shaughnessy, in the end he rejected all of them and returned to this larger, tragic story in which Richard's fatal flaw would be his loyalty. Even in the rushed rewrite of Lady Marjorie's affair, Hawkesworth took time to lay the groundwork for it: When Richard broaches the subject of faithfulness to his unfaithful wife, he does so obliquely, in terms of the loyalty he owes to Marjorie's family in return for their patronage, of the loyalty he owes to her and to her feelings—and ends by telling her that because of these loyalties he will not change sides to vote with the Liberals on the Education Bill. "I shall vote against the Bill, like the good Tory and the good husband which I hope I am. As you put it yourself, it is a simple question of loyalty—that's the most important thing in my life, much more than our passing whims—and passions."

Thus, Richard renounces his Liberal leanings, and Marjorie, getting the message, renounces her lover. In that context, just a sweet little tit-for-tat; in retrospect, though, a source of tragic irony— that his greatest virtue would become his tragic flaw.

Shaughnessy was making notes for still another irony, provided the series got that far into the century. Eventually Richard would lose both ways: not only when the Liberals sweep to power but again when they are swept *from* power, and from history. Because after Marjorie's death, he does change sides—just in time to become, like the Liberal party itself, an anachronism. On a field to be fought out between Labour and Tory he will inhabit a no-man's-land, out of sympathy with the Tories because he believes in a man's right to better himself, out of sympathy with Labour because he cannot accept the cheapening of values that makes a mockery of such betterment. So, just as he would end up homeless literally, he would also end up homeless politically and culturally.

8. James and Sarah fall in love and James talks to her of marriage, but she tells him, "It's no good; they won't have me." Distressed, he turns to Elizabeth for counsel; she, a *belle époque* version of a hippie, replies, "Why shouldn't you marry her? She's as good as you are." His rueful reply: "I'd have to resign

my commission in the regiment." (Surely, one of the great romantic speeches of all time.) Elizabeth asks, "Which is more important—love or the regiment?"

Love triumphs. James resigns his commission, takes a job in a bank, wedding bells ring out. . . . The End, Series I.

Or so it might have been.

To end with the wedding of James and Sarah would offer its advantages, Shaughnessy and Hawkesworth agreed. If LWT did not renew, Series I could stand on its own as an Edwardian Cinderella story. "And they lived happily ever after." If LWT did renew, Series II could pick up with the more workaday story of the marriage, for which Shaughnessy was already writing, ". . . the young couple will set up housekeeping in Dulwich; Lady Marjorie will send an under-houseparlormaid to be their cook-general. On her afternoon off Rose comes to tea and Sarah tells her she is having a baby. During their visit James comes home, depressed, and after Rose has gone, he tells her he has thrown up his job."

This marriage got as far as a rough draft of a script, then Hawkesworth and Shaughnessy took a long look—and withheld their blessing.

Why not, they pondered, end with the death of Edward VII? What could be a better frame for Edwardian vignettes?

What could be better, they decided, was to continue those vignettes another year—*if* they could get the necessary contract. So the series would end with Elizabeth marrying a poet. (In the States, where Series I and II were telescoped into one series, Elizabeth's wedding became Episode 3, and the series ended with the death of Edward VII.)

Though at the time there was no way of knowing, this decision to focus on Elizabeth instead of on James was most fortuitous, because Simon Williams (who played James) was not to be around for Series II. During those months while the Drama Controller was trying to dump the series, Williams had signed that contract with the West End theater.

The venal butler, the corrupt politician, the philandering husband, the malicious servants, the Cinderella wedding—any resemblance to persons or events in the *Upstairs, Downstairs* we finally saw is purely coincidental.

3

He thought he saw a Buffalo
Upon the chimney-piece:
He looked again and found it was
His Sister's Husband's Niece.

—Lewis Carroll, *Sylvie and Bruno*

SERIES II

Well, they had lost Simon Williams. So now, the back side of that script (literally) about James and Sarah setting up housekeeping in Dulwich was used for notes about Elizabeth and poet Laurence setting up housekeeping in Greenwich.

1. The staff of the newlyweds consists of Rose ("on loan" from Lady Marjorie), a cook, and a valet, Frank (later to become our Thomas). Shaughnessy's notes read: "Elizabeth is neurotic and discontented, as her new life with Laurence is nonexistent and her disillusionment with his vain and selfish character grows; converse to this, Rose, away from the conventional, restrictive atmosphere of belowstairs at Eaton Place under Hudson, begins to cast off her tight-lipped, spinsterish man-

ner and *live*. Working at close quarters with Frank, she soon falls under his spell and allows him into her bed. Thus, Elizabeth, who used to preach to her maidservant and friend Rose about freedom and illicit love, is suddenly the frustrated virgin, while her servant is singing and laughing about the house in the flush of an affair.

2. "Frank has finished with Rose now (though Rose does not know it), and turned his eye toward more ambitious goals. He suggests to Elizabeth that the purchase of a small, inexpensive coupe motorcar would give her more freedom of movement and enable her to go to London more often. Elizabeth jumps at the idea, seeing in a car her best chance of making a life for herself. She asks Frank to find her one. He does so and starts to take his young mistress out in it to teach her how to drive. He has added to his functions overnight the function of chauffeur and will soon add the function of Elizabeth's secret lover."

3. Elizabeth's marriage breaks up and she returns home to Number 165, bringing Rose with her. Roberts (Lady Marjorie's personal maid) sells the news of the breakup to *The Daily Mail,* and Richard threatens to sue Lord Northcliffe ("everyone did in those days"). Frank, nothing if not the charmer, has so impressed Lady Marjorie that she has asked him to join her staff as chauffeur; so, the happy ménage is still intact—except for Laurence, who had never really belonged. Soon, Elizabeth discovers she is pregnant. By—yes, Frank. A mess like this only Sir Geoffrey Dillon can work out. Pragmatist that he is, Dillon can always distinguish between problems that can be solved and those that can merely be kept a secret; with Southwold money he bribes the husband to agree never to deny paternity; the father, never to claim it. "The Bellamys will never know."

4. *Then*, just to keep the interest from flagging, Sarah, pregnant by James, returns to Number 165 to have her baby, and

promptly (very promptly) becomes the next object of Frank's attentions.

5. Then it is discovered that Frank is an ex-convict. . . .

6. *Meanwhile* . . . "A letter to Roberts from Lady Southwold's maid, read out at breakfast in the servants' hall, tells of a certain Violet Cooper, who used to be a laundrymaid at Southwold years ago, had an illegitimate child and later married a bank clerk in Salisbury. It seems Violet's husband died and she and her child have fallen on hard times. They've gone to live in the East End of London. Miss Hodges, Lady Southwold's maid, says in her letter that Violet wrote to the Southwolds for help and she thinks some money was sent. Miss Hodges adds that if any of the staff at Lady Marjorie's would care to help the woman, her address is 4a Blackwall Mansions, E. 6. Hudson seems a little put out by the news. He asks to see the letter.

"Later in the day Hudson comes to Richard to ask for the afternoon off. Richard is surprised to find Hudson has been drinking. Not his usual calm self. Hudson visits Violet in a horrible slum dwelling and finds her child (14 or 15 years old), which is his own, living in squalor. The mother is drunk and the child bruised. Hudson sets about to extricate the child from its mother and to get it into a decent school to ensure its future. This costs money. Hudson has overheard a share tip given to Bellamy at dinner by a visiting stockbroker. Hudson buys the shares. They slump. He loses all his savings and cannot help his daughter. He despairs and goes to pieces. The other servants have no idea what is wrong with him but they rally round and help and cover up for him. Richard tactfully makes inquiries and traces the matter back to the letter about Violet Cooper; he takes matters into his own hands and makes arrangements for the child's upbringing and education, while Violet, who is a hopeless alcoholic, is put into a home. Only when all is arranged does Hudson discover what Richard has done. His gratitude is overwhelming. The dour Scots butler weeps unashamedly as he leaves the morning room. The staff have rumbled what it was all about but never let on to Hudson that they ever knew."

The cast having been contracted months ahead, the replacement for this story still had to center on Hudson, et al.; so Shaughnessy came up with the story in which Hudson, to save his brother and sister-in-law the embarrassment of learning they have a butler in the family, masquerades as a political secretary.

7. Elizabeth becomes the mistress of an older man. . . .

The ending proposed for this lalapalooza of a series was to have been a family reunion for Lady Marjorie's fiftieth birthday. James would be home from India with a new fiancée (his year's contract in the West End theater coming then to an end); so we would have seen James standing beside his fiancée, "raising his glass to Sarah, the mother of his only-begotten, still-born child," Elizabeth raising hers to her new lover (the older man), Frank raising his to . . . Rose, his former ladylove? Elizabeth, whose child he has fathered? Or to Sarah, his current ladylove?

Into this scene of unabashed decadence Richard was to bring the news of the King's death. End of the Edwardian era. Good riddance, one would infer.

Shocking, quite. How in the name of logical sequence or even quantum leaps of faith did Shaughnessy get from *those* stories to *our* stories?

As nearly as one can reconstruct from the notebooks, he first wrote a plot. Just the bare situation. Then he explored the situation in terms of character, of social mores, relevant themes. Then he took that original straight, head-on situation and gave it an ambiguous shading, an ironic twist—an affair becoming an attraction; a dark secret, a small vanity. In the margin of his notes he would argue with a character's reaction; in one story line, for example, where he has given Hudson an uncharacteristic tolerance for an outburst of Edward's, Shaughnessy had written in the margin: "By all the rules of the series, Hudson should throw him out—neck and crop!"

Last, he would discard the original situation altogether. Rather like frying pork chops and adding onions and potatoes and seasoning and then throwing away the chops.

All along, of course, Hawkesworth was adding to the pot, giving it a stir.

And then the writer, whose job—in whatever medium—is to turn the simple, the blatant, the commonplace into the complex, the subtle, and the singular, would take over. By the time Rosemary Anne Sisson finished the script, the hanky-panky between Rose and Frank (now Thomas) came to no more than a game of blindman's buff. Elizabeth, alone in her bedroom, hears the laughing and shrieks of mirth and, like so many miserable people, is wildly resentful and—unconsciously—envious; putting the worst construction on it, she charges down to the kitchen, tells them she'll have no such goings-on, and dismisses them on the spot. Later, she falls into Rose's arms in tears, the same helpless "Miss Lizzy" that Rose had comforted, years ago, in her childhood.

In this final version Rose is still attracted to Thomas, but the story revolves around character, not incident. Rose has become an individual, not a bundle of stereotypical feminine sexual responses; her reactions to Thomas belong uniquely to her—an unworldly, uneducated orphaned woman of 1909, from a poor background, whose aunt had warned her about men; who, when asked by Elizabeth whether she "has ever . . . ?" answers, "Never, Miss Lizzy! Of course not! What you thinkin' of!" Though she is charmed and warmed by Thomas' attentions, all that she has been and is makes her prudent—and afraid. And a little regretful.

The story becomes one of the threads in the continuing theme "Will Rose ever leave the womb?" People like Sarah and Thomas and Alfred will have infinite appeal for her; their freedom and their sexuality will fascinate—and frighten—her. And always, in the end, bring out the Puritan in her. Even Gregory, the first time around.

As for Elizabeth and Thomas' affair in the household triangle, nothing remained. Not even so much as a stray glance.

There, however, the red pencil broke. Before it could scratch through a story of Laurence arranging for his publisher to "service" his frustrated wife. No wonder Nicola Pagett (who played Elizabeth) quit the series.

The actual ending for the second series, by the way, had the same family reunion, but with a different message: Elizabeth is there alone, forsaken by her lover; Thomas has occupied neither her bed nor Rose's. In this revised setting, the bearer of news of the King's death no longer comes onstage like a messenger of moral retribution.

Aside from having sidestepped most of those lurid pitfalls, what did Series II establish? Not much, really. "The second series slightly stretched us," Paul said; "we had exhausted the themes about Edwardian life; and, historically, the series covered a strange interim period, 1909–1910, where there was not much to latch on to; so we were into more random stories—a more fragmented series, really."

Just as well . . . because *eight of the thirteen episodes centered on characters who afterward quit the show.*

4

SERIES III

Series III was the moment of truth for *Upstairs, Downstairs*. They had lost Lady Marjorie, Elizabeth, Sarah, and Thomas—and were winning over the Drama Controller.

For it, Shaughnessy composed four sets of formats: two, ending with the Declaration of War; two, going through the war and ending with the Armistice.

From the first set of formats:

1. "James and Phyllis [the fiancée he brought from India to the family reunion] are married and living at 165. James is working at Jardines in the City, in a humble clerical job. Elizabeth has gone back to Laurence [who has, presumably, recovered or discovered his manhood]. Lady Southwold is dead, so Richard feels the time has come to cross the floor

of the House and sit on the Liberal benches. Conflict with Marjorie. Richard has come under the influence—intellectual rather than sexual—of a clever radical woman, a widow called Mrs. Raven, Eileen Raven. She is the widow of a Liberal MP whom Richard knew and now Richard calls on her. . . . Somehow his liaison is uncovered, for Richard and Mrs. Raven both receive most vicious and ugly poison-pen letters. . . . Richard employs a discreet private detective to try secretly to discover who wrote the letters. They are quickly traced to Rose. [!] It all comes out. Richard says his relationship is purely platonic, that she is helping him research his book (also a secret) on the life of Lord Grey, the Liberal Prime Minister of the 1830s. The servants are skeptical. Is it really a harmless liaison?"

2. After Lady Marjorie's death on the *Titanic,* Richard begins seeing Eileen Raven again. One evening he brings her, for the first time, for an open visit to Eaton Place; a furious row ensues, with James and Phyllis accusing her of trying to trap Richard into marriage, and Eileen responding that she is at least consoling Richard, which, she asserts, is more than they are doing.

3. Mrs. Bridges' friend, "companion to an ailing old lady in Eastbourne, is accused of murder—more precisely, of poisoning and chopping up the old lady and stuffing the pieces into the walls of the house.

4. On a foggy Christmas Eve, as the servants are returning from caroling, they discover that Ruby is no longer with them. One minute she was there, the next she has vanished. Lost in the fog? "Oh, that girl!" Mrs. Bridges grumbles. Time passes, and Ruby does not show up—something must have happened to her. Jack the Ripper? Panic. The police are called. No sign. Bedtime—and still no Ruby. After the house quiets down and everyone is in bed, they hear noises: Ruby, having drunk too much wine at the Christmas dinner,

"got took" during the caroling, had to rush back to Number
165 to the outdoor WC—and got locked in.

Enough of all that, Hawkesworth and Shaughnessy decided. No
more of Phyllis. And no more of Eileen Raven.

Shaughnessy returns to his notebook. And writes a second set of
formats.

There will still be a quarrel between Richard and Lady Marjorie,
but not over a woman. As in the episode of Marjorie's infidelity, it
will be over politics—once again Richard has announced his intention of switching to the Liberal party, and once again he forgoes
his convictions. (Ergo, no poison-pen letters by Rose.)

Enter: Miss Forrest—Richard's secretary, our Hazel. Then, for
a few episodes at least, the stories are recognizable: James courts
Hazel, marries Hazel, and then . . .

Where the brain-storming for Series II began with the lurid, here
it proceeded with the macabre; after scratching the idea for chopping
up the old lady, Shaughnessy comes up with:

1. Alfred, the footman who ran away with the German baron
   in Series II, returns, a fugitive. He has murdered a child.
   (He will, in the final version, have murdered his lover—a
   mite less horrible, perhaps.)

2. Richard is pursued by a "bridge-playing, predatory society
   woman." (In the final version, she becomes an adventuress,
   an imposter posing as a friend of Marjorie's—a dubious
   improvement.)

3. A new housemaid, who claims to be a psychic, announces
   that there is an evil presence in the wall of her attic room
   and that she will not spend another night there. The younger
   servants, impressionable and gullible, work themselves into
   such a state of terror that the work of the house cannot go
   on; so, Hazel, to forestall the rising hysteria, calls in a builder
   to tear out the wall. An act tantamount, in the young ser-

vants' eyes, to challenging God to strike her dead. Hazel's plan backfires, and the servants achieve a creepy credibility—and vindication—when, inside the wall, the builder discovers a disused chimney and in the chimney the skeleton of a small child. A chimney sweep of Victorian days. Now, Hazel plays it their way—she calls in the local parson to exorcise the house.

4. "Ruby gets the push for stealing and lying." (A touch of larceny in Ruby—a notion that will be put on the shelf until the very end of the five series. "It was John's idea—one of his best," Shaughnessy said. In the very last moments of the last episode, when we are deep in sniffles, when Mrs. Bridges, sobbing, is being helped out the back entrance by Hudson, Ruby—up in her room—slyly confides to Rose that she is going along with Hudson and Mrs. Bridges to their boardinghouse only because she has designs on taking it over. "They can't live forever, can they?")

5. Rose falls in love with an Australian sergeant, on leave from France. (Yes, war has been declared, but in this format, it gets short shrift—half a series.) The young man, it seems to Hudson, has a very long leave; so, he decides to do some discreet investigating—and discovers that the sergeant is really a private and, moreover, a deserter. This presents Hudson with unpalatable options: harboring a deserter in the house and thereby compromising Bellamy, who is Minister of Recruiting; reporting him and thereby becoming responsible for his death by firing squad. The outline ends with this enigmatic line: "Hudson and Mrs. Bridges find their own solution."

An afterthought is penciled in—"Her lover is not only a deserter but is found to have a wife and four children back in Brisbane."

In the reworking, as we know, what comes between Rose and her Australian is not some revelation from his past but Rose herself. Not circumstance but character. Offered freedom and new horizons, she sees only strangeness—and retreats to the familiar, back to Eaton Place, hopeless and restrictive though it may be. Another thread in the continuing story "Will Rose ever leave the womb?"

6. "Hazel and Richard are now faced with the awful truth that they are in love and the situation is becoming almost unbearable. Richard, widowed and lonely, is under the same roof as his daughter-in-law, while his son is at the front. At the height of this crisis a telegram comes, reporting James 'missing and believed killed.' " Now Richard is torn asunder by grief and guilt and the realization that it is now both possible and impossible for him and Hazel to marry. "Then comes the follow-up wire. James was found in no-man's-land, gassed and badly wounded in the arm. He is in a field hospital and is too ill to be evacuated back further." Hazel, tortured by guilt, knows she must go to him. "His desire to help Hazel reach her wounded husband (and his wounded son) causes Richard to abuse his position in the War Office and sign various passes that enable Hazel to enter a forward military area and thus breach security. The bitter war between the generals and politicians is exemplified by the reaction of a general who hates politicians and has a grudge against Richard; he causes a question to be asked of the War Minister in the House: 'Can the Minister say the Undersecretary should be allowed to provide a pass for his daughter-in-law to enter a restricted military zone to visit her wounded husband, when this privilege is not granted to the wives of other officers or serving men?' The press take it up. There is a major scandal. Lloyd George is furious and Richard is carpeted. In his own conscience he acted more out of his love for Hazel than with concern for his own son. He offers Lloyd George his resignation. It is accepted and Richard is out of office and in disgrace." (Thus endeth Plan Number 4 for Richard's downfall.)

7. Georgina, at the train station helping to greet the wounded

soldiers returning from France, meets a young officer on a stretcher (Billy Garland). . . . They will begin seeing each other and will become engaged.

By the time this gets to the television viewers, the young soldier will be too far gone for romance: Georgina lights a cigarette for him, puts it in his mouth, he tries to thank her—and dies.

8. James is recuperating at an officers' hospital in the West Country . . . Hazel is staying in Bath to be near him. "Richard is at his lowest ebb . . . he feels old and lonely and beaten." Word comes to him that James has had his arm amputated.

9. "James is home now, minus his arm. Pale and quiet but showing signs of coming around slowly. Hazel devotes her time to him. . . . A terrible epidemic of flu breaks out and most of the staff are struck down. Hazel and Georgina are forced to take over in the kitchen . . . and Richard says one has to admire the guts of the young women of his family, who take the helm and steer through the crisis. One day, he feels, young society ladies may have to cook in kitchens. 'I sometimes feel your mother is well out of it. How she would have hated the disruption of the house and the idea of her daughter-in-law down there cooking the vegetables and taking trays up to the servants' rooms. It would have horrified her.' James smiles and has to agree." A far cry from the scene *we* remember—when Hazel was helping Ruby because Mrs. Bridges was sick, and James behaved as if she had triggered Armageddon: "Put that whatever-it-is away and go upstairs this minute where you belong. . . . You are responsible for running his house with *dignity,* as Mother did, from the morning room, not messing about the kitchen like a scullery maid." The flu will prove fatal to Violet (who is to be exchanged, anyway, for our Daisy), and it will be

Hudson's lot to have to write Edward, at the front, and let him know.

For the last episode, which was to have brought an end to the saga of Eaton Place, this is proposed:

10. "Armistice . . . The house is dirty and covered in dust. Rooms unlived in. People are starting to talk of the 'world fit for heroes to live in.' But there is unemployment. Ex-servicemen are begging and playing barrel organs in the London squares. . . . James is suffering from lung trouble and Hazel is told that he must have mountain air, so they decide to go and live in Switzerland, in the Alps above Zurich. Richard is made a peer in the Birthday Honours and feels his indiscretion in the war has been forgiven. Perhaps General Mansfield, who caused his downfall, calls to congratulate him and the two men make up their difference.

"Things are not the same now at Eaton Place. Hudson and Mrs. Bridges have gone, realizing that things are never going to be the same, that the old days have gone—and that they are getting on and tired. They have pooled their savings and bought an old boardinghouse; [this idea was the only one that was kept] Edward, demobilized and mourning Violet, after trying hard to find work in the cold outside world, has been forced to try for a job in his old profession of domestic service. But he is older and wiser now, so Richard says he will give him references as a butler. Sir Geoffrey Dillon comes to call and we find that Richard is very hard up [Dillon's presence always did spell trouble] and cannot afford to go on living at Eaton Place. Dillon, always practical, suggests that, since Georgina, his niece by marriage, is an heiress under her mother's will (the *Titanic* left Georgina very well off) and is about to marry young Billy Garland, who is well connected, the young couple might well take over Eaton Place. So Richard takes rooms in Hill Street, Mayfair, where he will live out his days and write his memoirs, surrounded by souvenirs of Marjorie and photographs of Southwold and Elizabeth as a child on her pony, and James on the tennis court.

"The young Garlands become the new master and mistress of 165 Eaton Place and retain Rose as housekeeper, Edward as their young butler. . . . Billy stands for Parliament in the by-election and gets in. The Garlands will be leaders of the new postwar society, and once more Number 165, occupied by a Southwold lady and a young and rising MP, will come alive, this time to the sounds of the Charleston on the gramophone, pajama parties, and cocktail soirees. Along the street comes a new under-housemaid for an interview. She is new to service. She rings the front-door bell; Edward, in his butler's tailcoat, opens it. He allows the girl to enter by the front door for her interview. Things have changed, yet in a sense history is beginning to repeat itself. *'Plus ça change, plus c'est la même chose.'* "

For those who may not remember, in Scene 1, Episode 1, Series I, Sarah, also new to service, arrived for her interview at the front door—and was brusquely ordered by Hudson to go to the servants' entrance.

Then *this* ending is proposed:

James not only loses an arm—he is gassed, he suffers head injuries, his speech is impaired, and his motor reflexes are palsied.

The household at Eaton Place is at a very low ebb. Daisy is down with flu, so is Rose. The only cheerful person in the house is Georgina, who has fallen hopelessly in love with a young Grenadier captain with the Military Cross—Hugh Preston. . . . There is bombing every night, many of the windows are broken, and there is dust and debris everywhere. Hudson, who is aging a bit now, suffers from a mild heart attack. . . . Alice Hamilton [to become our Virginia Hamilton] is seeing a lot of Richard. They dine together at the Ritz and Richard asks her to marry him. She accepts. She comes to Eaton Place and helps by going to the kitchen and helping cook for the flu victims. Eaton Place is a sickroom. Hazel is with James at Somerby [Bunny Newbury's estate, which is now a convalescent hospital for officers] wheeling him on the terrace in his wheelchair. The news of the Armistice comes . . . *James can hardly take it in.* [Italics mine.]

Georgina marries Hugh Preston at the Guards Chapel. Hudson and Mrs. Bridges decide to go to Richard and warn him of their intention to retire, to marry, and to run a boardinghouse. Richard and Alice go to Paris for the Peace Conference at Versailles. Hazel and James go off to Switzerland, where, overlooking the Lake of Geneva, James will spend the rest of his days in a sanatorium [recommended by Dillon—of course]. Hazel will look after him. Daisy and Edward, now demobbed, go off to look for work and a new home in which to bring up their forthcoming child—they are determined not to go back into service. . . . Dillon suggests Eaton Place should be made over to Georgina and her husband. . . . Rose will stay on as housekeeper . . . she is quite gray now and wears a black, plain dress. Her mind is full of memories, as she stands in the hall, looking up the stairs. Daisy and Edward ring the bell and ask to see Hazel. They are told she is living in Switzerland now, and that Miss Georgina is mistress of the house. Daisy and Edward cannot find work, great unemployment—may they come back into service? Georgina and her new husband engage them as Butler and Cook. . . . Rose gives the young couple tea in the servants' hall and life goes on. . . .

Luckily, LWT moved faster than when they lost James to India—a hero drooling in a wheelchair could never have got us through twenty-six more episodes. "Hold back the war," they said; "make it into a series all its own."

So these stories, too, were scratched, and an entirely new series began—the pre-war series.

Rose will meet someone . . . a man miles above her in social station takes her out—or even away—perhaps to the wilds of Cornwall, and it looks as if it is the greatest Cinderella story in history.

. . . She is dressed in fine clothes, dined and wined and treated like a lady. For a whole forty-eight hours, she is lifted from her humdrum world and lives in a sort of fool's paradise. *Retour à l'aube.* But Rose finds the man, for all his wealth and position, a sad, lonely creature, more in need of help and pity than someone she can be swept away by. The bubble bursts, and she is back at Eaton Place, with her private memory.

As for James:

James starts drinking and gambling. One evening when he thinks he has the house to himself, he is caught in his bedroom by Rose, sleeping with an actress, in Hazel's bed. James tries desperately to silence Rose, who is shocked and enraged. She admires Hazel and respects her, and James has again shown his worst side, weak, effete, easily tempted. The actress is sent packing in a taxi and James comes out with it in spite of himself: "What's a man to do when he knows his father's in love with his wife? There, now you know. . . ." Great remorse by James. He shouldn't have said it to a servant. Rose is very thoughtful. James threatens her cruelly not to speak. Rose broods. Hazel returns and shortly afterward her parents come to London to tea at Eaton Place. James is rather rude and offhand to them. Hazel tries to conceal that there is anything wrong. Richard is all charm and good manners and Hazel's mother remarks what a charming man he is. Her daughter just nods. She can hardly tell her mother she is in love with her father-in-law.

The difference between Eaton Place and Peyton Place, it might be noted, is that Peyton Place's plotting stopped where Eaton Place's started.

A later episode:

James is openly accusing Hazel of having an affair with his father. She cries and denies it. She is fond of Richard and admires him, but that is all. James and his father have the most bitter row. James behaves abominably. He has more money than his father, who only lives at the house on his charity. James more or less tells his father to clear out. Richard is deeply hurt. He will, of course, look for rooms. He has no wish to stay where he is not wanted. Hazel is furious with James for treating his father like that. The row upsets the servants and sides are taken. Richard, driven to extremes by James' fury, born of his guilt and self-knowledge that he is not worthy of Hazel, resorts to reminding James of his dead mother and what she would have thought of him." [A touché that Shaughnessy will hold on to and use, two series later, in the fatal row preceding James' suicide—it will be the one remark, James will tell Georgina, that he cannot forgive his father for.] "James, deathly pale, slams out of the room. The evening paper comes. Archduke Franz Ferdinand has been assassinated at Sarajevo. Richard stares out of the window—it is a hot night. Outside the distant rumble of thunder.

[Richard and James will have this row—but it will be over James' treatment of Hazel after her miscarriage.]

In the event that the reader may by now be so thoroughly confused he can no longer remember how Series III *did* end: It was with the servants' outing at the seashore, where the newsboys are shouting, "War Latest! Invasion of France!" Where Daisy and Edward are falling in love and Mrs. Bridges out of love (with her fishmonger), where Hudson, at the outdoor music hall, recites:

> *"There's a one-eyed yellow idol to the north of Khatmandu,*
> *There's a little marble cross below the town,*
> *There's a broken-hearted woman tends the grave of Mad Carew,*
> *And the yellow god forever gazes down."*

His recital is interrupted by the news that Belgium has asked England to come to her aid, and the audience—jubilant—breaks out singing "Rule, Britannia."

The actual declaration of war comes afterward, with all of them back at Eaton Place—after James has left, happy as a schoolboy, to join his regiment; Richard and Hazel are in the morning room; the crowds in the streets are chanting, "We want war! We want war!"

RICHARD: Well, they're going to get their war, poor wretches.

HAZEL: Is it going to be very bad?

RICHARD: Very bad. And for very long. At least, that's what I think. And so does Kitchener.

HAZEL: It's extraordinary—but I feel a tremendous sense of relief, as if a spring had been released somewhere inside me.

RICHARD: James is not the only one who needed a war to cast out his devil. Thousands of people all over Europe are marching up and down, happy and joyful, screaming their heads off for it—all praying to the same God for victory. Poor God! He's got a hard time ahead.

HAZEL: Perhaps it was his idea. At least we can say we are going in to help our friends.

RICHARD: Poor little Belgium! Oh yes, we can beat our breasts with a clear conscience, but there's a good practical reason as well—Antwerp still is a pistol pointed at England's head.

HUDSON: (entering with champagne and glasses) It's five minutes to eleven. (setting them down) Shall I open the bottle, sir?

RICHARD: No, thank you. But do have a drink downstairs—if you feel like celebrating.

HUDSON: Thank you, sir. (leaves)

RICHARD: Last night Sir Edward Grey, looking out across the park, said, "The lights are going out all over Europe. We shall not see them lit again in our lifetime." (pause) I am too old for war, Hazel. This means the end of that pleasant order of things I have known and lived and loved. The end forever.

HAZEL: (reaching out to his hand) I do see. (Georgina and Billy Laynton come into the room, in full evening dress, as excited as though they had just won the sweepstakes.)

GEORGINA: Hello . . . the whole of London has gone mad! We have been at the most gorgeous war party at the Ritz

—everyone was there—and we met a nice colonel who promised to help Billy get a commission in the Grenadiers. And I've come to a great decision—I am going to be a nurse so that I can be with the Army. . . .

RICHARD: Champagne, please, Billy. (Billy turns to open the bottle.) I hate to dampen your ardor, but I hope neither of you has anything to do with this war. You are far too young. (Billy pours the champagne. Outside the crowd begins to sing "Pomp and Circumstance"; Richard raises his glass. . . .) I refuse to drink a toast to war. From battle and murder and from sudden death, good Lord, deliver us. (They raise their glasses—Richard and Hazel, solemn; Georgina and Billy, with suppressed excitement.)

Downstairs, as Rose pours the beer, Edward and Daisy and Ruby come in the back entrance—like Georgina and Billy, filled with holiday excitement.

EDWARD: Mr. Hudson, you should have seen the crowds outside Buckingham Palace—they were all singing and shouting at the tops of their voices—

HUDSON: Help yourselves to some beer.

RUBY: We saw the King and Queen and the Prince of Wales come out on the balcony—

EDWARD: And we saw Mr. Churchill and Mr. Asquith and Lloyd George—as clear as anything . . . and just as—

HUDSON: Quiet, Edward— (The sound of cannons and church bells and cheering. Hudson stands.) This is an historic moment in the history of our country and our empire—we are now at war with Germany. (removes glasses) Our cause is a righteous one. (raising his mug of beer) May the Lord, mighty in battle, give us victory. (They drink.) God save the King.

ALL: God save the King.

The camera goes from face to face—Hudson, with visions of glory; Edward, excited; Daisy, in tears; Ruby, serious; Rose, sickened.

The crowd sings.

5

Steady as she goes . . .

—Ship captain's phrase

SERIES IV

After all those trial runs for including the war in Series III, doing the actual war series (IV) was a breeze.

The early drafts, in fact, differ in only two principal ways from the ones we saw: Elizabeth was to have returned from America for one episode; and James was to have been at the Officers' Hospital when Hazel dies—instead of sitting at home, indifferent.

6

Since now at length my fate I know.

—Robert Browning, *The Last Ride Together*

SERIES V

By now the writers know they are headed for Maidenhead. All else was diversionary.

Of the diversions proposed and rejected we need take no notice —except for these three:

1. "To better herself, Ruby goes into service with a clergyman in Sidcup as a cook-general. (God help his Reverence.)"
2. Ruby marries the milkman.
3. "The Prince of Wales comes to dinner, fancies Virginia, and in contrast with Edward VII's evening of bridge, we have the carpet rolled up and dancing to the gramophone—the Charleston, the Black Bottom. The servants are thrilled, for the Prince of Wales comes downstairs to congratulate Mrs.

Bridges on the dinner and she is able to tell him she cooked for his grandfather in this very kitchen in 1909."

Now, to Maidenhead.

In the last notes on the war, Shaughnessy wrote, "James will not be killed in the war, but it will destroy him." Now he must decide—how? when? why?

Shaughnessy, for whatever reasons (logic not being among them), first decided—*where*. ". . . he is found with his service revolver in his hand in a Maidenhead hotel."

As to *when* . . . in the middle of the series. "In 1926, after the General Strike."

(Under this plan, the series itself was to end in May 1929, on the night "the second Labour Government in British history returned to office," signaling "a new order of things." Nice, that.)

And last—*how*? By what steps would James be brought to that hotel? The first draft shows the usual bit of overkill: James loses a by-election, ". . . shifts from job to job . . . falls briefly in love with a married woman whose husband refuses to divorce . . . loses all his money, takes to drink and becomes a wreck."

Downhill all the way.

With worse to come. On the second draft:

James, still shattered by his experiences in the war, depressed, lonely and becoming embittered, loses what little money he has in some shady City venture into which he has been conned by a brash friend of Georgina's and is forced—at Dillon's suggestion—to transfer the deed of the house to his wealthy stepmother, Virginia, who will thus become the new mistress of 165. James will have his own bedroom and dressing-room and a small sitting room of his own upstairs.

So, in an ironic reprise of the story that made Richard a lodger in his son's house, James becomes a lodger in his stepmother's house.

And the third draft:

James has met up with two men, both ex-officers, who have a get-rich-quick scheme requiring some capital investment. James has meanwhile lost most of his capital and cannot invest himself. . . . But he is keen on the scheme—something to do with secondhand cars—so he privately speaks to Rose about it. [Her nest egg of £3000 left her by Gregory.] He persuades her that she can double her money if she invests it in the business. She is wary and cautious but James persuades her, telling her not to mention it to Lord or Lady Bellamy or Miss Georgina. It is essential the business project remain a secret.

The project goes wrong and James finds he has lost Rose's savings and cannot replace the money. He is bitterly ashamed. He broods on it. Everything he has turned his hand to has gone wrong. Later on, the scheme comes to fruition and James's partners try to get in touch with him. Rose's shares in the business are up in value. Nobody knows where James is. Then comes the news that he has been found in his bedroom at a small riverside hotel near Maidenhead, shot in the mouth by his own service revolver. He has left a note to his father, apologizing for the shame. "I came here to do it, not to make a mess of my room."

Who, at this point, would have wept for Hecuba?

No one, they decided.

If we were to grieve for James, we must hope for him—and with him, for he too must have hope.

So, instead of acting out *The Rake's Progress*, James *will* fight a good campaign in the by-election, he *will* keep the house and share it with Richard and Virginia and her children, he will *not* fall in with Georgina's fast friends, he *will* make money on the stock market, he *will* return from America high and confident; yet all his hopes, and ours for him, will prove false. Just as he had failed in his marriage and in his hopes of winning Georgina, he will fail in politics, fail his best friend by having an affair with his wife, and fail in his responsibility to Rose by losing her money (though not to further his own schemes). But despite all that, he does not end up a shiftless, impoverished drunk whose death does everyone a favor.

(One thing Shaughnessy kept—unmodified: "I came here to do it, not to make a mess of my room at home.")

Of all this plotting, Simon Williams (James) knew nothing. He was still hoping he and Georgina would get it together. Nor was he alone. Bill Bain (a director) went to Hawkesworth and asked, "Will James and Georgina marry?" Hawkesworth answered, "Oh, good God, no! No!" But told him no more.

Not that knowing made it easier. . . . "It's all very well knowing James is going to die, but the wretched writer still has to write the bloody play!" Hawkesworth said, "He can't just have James sitting in his room loading his gun or tying nooses for three acts.

"Jeremy was always keen on having James die," Hawkesworth told me, "so I said, 'Right, then, I commission you to write the episode.' "

165 Eaton Place goes to war.

ward teaches soldiering to Ruby. (Episode 2, "News from the Front.")

Edward leaves for the front. (Episode 4, "Women Shall Not Weep.")

...ose becomes a bus conductorette. (Episode 6, "Home Fires.")

Rose and Gregory. (Episode 6, "Home Fires.")

James and Georgina, at war cemetery in France. (Episode 7, "If You Were the Only Girl in the World.")

Home on leave. (Episode 8, "The Glorious Dead.")

At field hospital in France.
(Episode 11, "Missing Presumed Killed.")

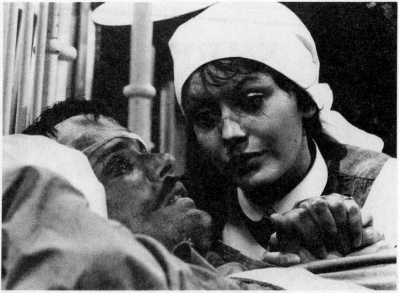

Georgina nurses James. (Episode 11, "Missing Presumed Killed.")

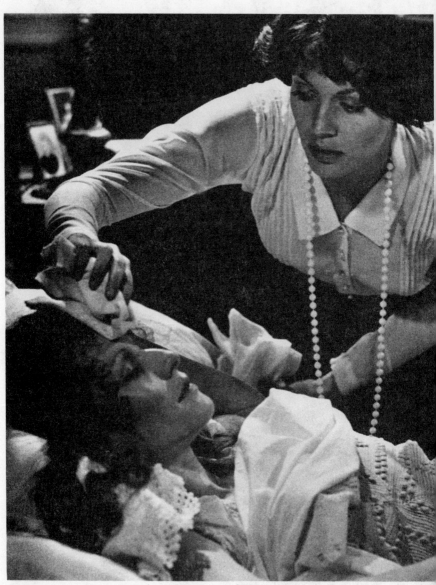

Georgina nurses Hazel. (Episode 13, "Peace out of Pain.")

PART 3

The Muse
with Her Sleeves
Rolled Up

(Addenda for the hard-core aficionado)

1

Who killed Cock Robin?

—Mother Goose Rhymes

So James is going to die and Jeremy Paul is to be the hit man. Episode 15, Final series.

Plotting James' emotional graph: "I couldn't let him just mope around for three acts," Paul explained. "I decided he would start with a high, returning from America successful and confident; then there would be the stock-market crash, then the loss of Rose's money, then the final rejection by Georgina."

There was one problem. The way he had it planned, it was going to leave no one for James to talk to in his last hours: He was to have a row with his father, he was to lose Rose's money, he was to be turned down by Georgina. And since soliloquies have fallen from fashion, the only way he could give us a glimpse into James' mind in those crucial hours was to have him talk to *someone*. But to whom?

"Somewhere along I remembered that in the years that had gone before, James had a propensity for opening up his heart to young women employed in the house." (Sarah, the under-houseparlormaid;

Hazel, his father's secretary). "Daisy wouldn't do . . ." (And Ruby was out of the question!)

"Finally I had the idea of bringing in a *new* housemaid. So I asked Freddie, 'Can I bring in a new character?' And he said, 'Yes,' and we were off."

This would bring James full circle, back to his past.

And that is how it came to pass that one last itinerant housemaid appeared at Number 165.

In the process of the writing, the metaphors would come—ghosts, closed doors, souvenirs, photographs, and letters (eleven correspondents, culminating in that last letter of all, the suicide letter). The souvenirs alone will tell a story: Rose's only souvenir is Gregory's money; Georgina has kept *no* souvenirs, feeling the future is all that counts; James has kept everything—the past is all he has, and he has no one to share it with but a new under-houseparlormaid, and no one to leave it to.

Here, then, is a transcript of Paul's notes and drafts for the suicide episode. Except for the exigencies of typesetting, they are exactly as they appear in his notebook. This key may prove helpful:

1. //———//   Lines that Paul had crossed out.
2. Small Print   Paul's marginal notes, changes, and additions.
3. *   My insertions and explanations.

2

Jeremy Paul's Working Notes for "All the King's Men"

Richard
Virginia
James
Georgina
Hudson
Mrs. B.
Rose
Daisy
~~New Footman?~~
New Houseparlourmaid
~~Dillon~~
Ruby?

panatrope
cabinet gramophone

Autumn 1929
Early September

James' Suicide

Story and background: James returns "high" after trip to America(Aust?). Attracted to frenetic world of bankers, business, social whirl (cutting out the emptiness underneath of his life in England). Drinking also. Over-exuberant. Household slightly rocked by his energy. He stayed with Elizabeth, saw her world. The success she's made of it. On return it emphasizes his own failure. The shimmering American world holds him into act one—he has pitched a massive amount of his own money into the American stockmarket. Persuades Rose to put <u>all</u> hers in his cause. Acts as her broker. Gets her to sign papers. When the crash comes, she's lost all - and he hasn't enough to pay her back.

J- "wiped out"

Terrific row with Richard. James has broken a taboo-- (money and servants). Richard invokes the memory of Marjorie. Richard says you've lured innocent Rose into your get-rich-quick, fly-by-night schemes. What would she have done if she <u>had</u> the money--her place is here. Under our protection. She was all right as she was. Now she has nothing and we can't afford to make it up to her.

Richard accuses James of lacking guts & moral fibre! This stings

Rose is made hysterical by loss. Not for money--but for deeper emotional reasons. Her safe, cozy relationship with dead Gregory has been swept away. She is alone, broke, suddenly frightened of the future. It might seem <u>her</u> life is the one in jeopardy. Hudson seeks to understand, comfort (also Mrs. B.). She's safe here. But Rose revolts at this. She's lost her independence. She's trapped forever. Bound to the house. She goes out all night. They fear for her. Where the hell is she? She's left her things. She just walks about. Returns next morning. No one knows where she's been. Perhaps no one ever will know. Has she had a man---speculation? As the house rocks----Rose's crisis passes. She is becalmed. Ready to continue.

Jewelry for Va.
Sable for G.
Silk dressing gown - R
Macy's - New York

This will provide the necessary diversion from James' growing paranoia.

During the fitful night of Rose missing, he is consumed with guilt and shame. And it's through this night that the moment of reckoning comes.

It probably comes in a major scene with Georgina. Shattered by his failures, he turns for a last hope of comfort to Georgina.

The beautiful irony of the scene will be that Georgina believes that she is bringing him round. Rebuilding his dreams. But as a <u>sister</u>--and he reaches out to her as an (impossible) lover. She is now engaged and hopefully settled after the frenetic times. She wants James to share this optimism. She believes she has succeeded.

Rose returns.
(Hudson has been angry about her. The number of times over the years she has claimed to be trapped--she has always been free to go--especially after the money. She has always <u>chosen</u> to stay. He wants to chide her, but Mrs. B, understanding her better, warns him not to. It's not the time.)

(
? (
(

Simply took a bus ride to Ilford & back.

Rose comes back, mysterious, as if nothing's happened. Virginia, who has been distraught, summons her. She is prepared to be angry. Rose looks surprised. It was all a misunderstanding. She has stayed with some friends of Gregory's in Potter's Bar, the Matthews. She thought she had told Hudson. Virginia doesn't believe her, neither should we—but we have to accept it. She seems none the worse.

Or, simply went too far!

Virginia's other concern is (not so much James as) Richard's explosion of anger at James which he feels was unjustified. So does Richard in retrospect (it was a father's disappointment in his favorite son, not living up to promise--a familiar syndrome). Richard wearily wants to make it up. But how? Invokes Virginia's imagination on the matter. She suggests a peace offering.

(
(
? (
(

A present. She has seen a painting. A battle scene. The Guards in an earlier engagement (check). It will soothe him. Richard blesses her and agrees to buy it

(
(
(

with what little money is available. A pre-Christmas present. (Nice, this, if James has been showering them with presents earlier.)

J - in a bow tie

Meanwhile James is in his room. By now the worst has been done to set his frame of mind. His father's loss of faith in him. (Total) (The inability to love--symbolized by Georgina, who has found her happiness. The sense he has of her patronizing him. A useless, cuddly thing--not to be thrown away, out of sentimental value. Her rejection of him. No recognition of his true needs. As if she didn't know him at all, was talking of someone else.)

It's almost all been said. All that is left is his mother and the war itself.

He methodically sorts out his private letters. A clear-out. He knows what he is going to do.

And we must have an awful suspicion now.

Letters from Georgina in the war
        from Elizabeth
        from Marjorie
        from Hazel

What would he have kept?

Photographs of private life. And then to his Regimental drawers. Various things. (Belt and cap) amongst which is, as a matter of course, the service revolver. Which he scarcely looks at. During which, the new young housemaid comes in. She is young, pretty, full of him (a vision and copy of Sarah, really). Having a clear-out, sir?

JAMES (totally in command) Yes, I am. Want to help? And she does. He watches. Allows her to burn his old letters. Unable really to do it himself.

> JAMES Awful, isn't it, keeping old stuff?
> HMAID I agree, sir. This pile here, sir?
>   (the photos go into the fire)

He shows her a picture of Marjorie. She admires her beauty. Most beautiful lady I've ever seen, sir. I've heard them talk about her o' course. And as she talks about his mother, he stares at <u>her</u>—they are flirting. The girl knows it and she's enjoying herself. Know she's throwing away old love letters. They can laugh about it. He packs a small bag. We don't see what. Then he goes. She looks round. He is gone. The door open. The letters burn.

Now possibly down the stairs--and various contacts are made. It's mid-evening, November. Virginia, pleased with her peace-making plans, calls him through open door—he hasn't meant to go in. She's alone. Where's father? Having a bath. Do you want to talk? No doesn't matter. It was nothing. Virginia reassures him, starts to try to explain, then breaks off as James
//~~She feels the painting will do the talking.~~//
seems uninterested. Distracted?

perhaps not
(
(
(
(
(
(
(
(
(

So the crucial figures in this drama, Georgina and Richard, are absent. James meets Hudson in the hall. H. reassures him that Rose has quite recovered from her crisis. She's back in harness. James says he's glad to hear it. Says he won't be in to supper. And not to stay up—he may be late. He's taking the car.

> H. Very good, sir. Good night, sir.
> J. Goodbye, Hudson.

(Hudson only recollects this afterwards—James goes out, as housemaid comes downstairs—James appears to see her, but says nothing. Goes. Housemaid stares

admiringly after James. Hudson orders her sharply
below.

(
(
(
? (
(

That night, after everyone has gone to bed, Georgina
returns late, rapturously happy. (maybe meets Rose?)
Passes James' room. Looks in. It's empty. Rather
tidy.

Is it about Rose?

Rose enters

Shocked household

Ring on doorbell. About midnight. Two policemen.
Hudson opens door. Sense of mystery. They ask to
see Lord Bellamy--he comes down, with Virginia.
The news is broken. James has shot himself in the
mouth in a Maidenhead hotel. There is a letter. Richard holds up—as policemen go. Hudson sends for
brandy. Virginia calm. Georgina comes down. Richard, led to bed, collapses weeping on the stairs.

Next morning, downstairs. Stunned. Why did he do
it? Rose blames herself in some way.

Richard, alone in James' room. His silent grief. Virginia and Georgina—best to leave him alone.

Virginia, fending off journalists.

End on Richard.

James' letter:

Dear Father   Please don't blame yourself for what
I'm doing. Everything you said about me was true.
I have always felt I was living on borrowed time since
that moment at Passchendaele when a German officer
could have shot me—but declined to. I have felt
useless since then. Merely a spectator. I can't go on
like this. I ask your forgiveness for the shame I bring
on you and the family. Please try to see it as a noble
action. An officer's way out when he can no longer

do justice to himself or the men under his command.
I came here to do it, not to make a mess of my room
and upset the servants //~~more than necessary~~.//

Forgive me   James

FIRST PLOTTINGS

1. <u>Int</u>. <u>Hall</u>. Day. Edward enters with 2 bags. Goes
back for more. James enters, alone, jazzy suit—
bow tie. ^{from M.R.} Back from U.S. Mary comes //~~down the
stairs~~,// they meet briefly. Hudson arrives downstairs, breathless. Edward brings in more cases.
Insists he, not Hudson, take them upstairs. Mary
sent to run bath. Hudson tells James the whereabouts of V, R, and G. There will be a dinner
party.

R - New govt.

J - been away 8
months?

Daisy - picking up
vibrations of money.

2. <u>M.R.</u> Presents given. Virginia, jewelry. Richard,
silk dressing gown. Feeling of James "high" which
they share. V. goes to change dress to match
jewelry. R. and J., brief warm moment. News
of G.'s engagement. Is it serious, is it a good
thing, etc. G. enters—wildly pleased to see Jumbo.
Receives her sable fur ecstatically.

Possibly, briefly
Mrs. B's preparation,
favorite dishes,
excitement

Edw. & D - H, M
subject of easily
acquired wealth,
without working for
it.

3. Wild scenes, downstairs, of enthusiasm. //~~Brief~~//
Note Mary, as a "listener." Rose and Edward
about V.'s jewelry. Is he rich? H.'s knowledge of
American wealth. The idea of Rose putting her
money in with James. Firmly rejected by Rose
and Hudson—against Edward and Daisy.

Laughs and possibly a
brief moment about
Marjorie. No—this
has to be private, to
Georgina

4. Dinner—the "colour" James gives us of America.
Enjoyment of good wine. News of Elizabeth's life.
The ethic of making-money. James' understand-

able boasting—their jokey caution. Toasts and celebration. James seems in very good form.

5. James enters his room. And we realize he's sober. The room makes him lonely, reminds him of emptiness he has been at pains to conceal. The staring dead faces.   It's a kind of shock.

James' renewed energy - time to change decor, etc.

Ghosts. G. enters like one. Startles him. In the sable fur. She talks of love. Asks him about American widows. They must look after each other in the absences of their loved ones. They agree to ride together in the morning.

In his case, the invented widow and the dead mother and wife.

6. James wakes late. Mary has brought him breakfast. (as another apparition) The house's orders were <u>not</u> to wake him. G. has gone gaily riding alone. (sense of <u>not</u> needing him). James annoyed.

Just a little but he persuades her to give him the lot.

Does he ask her what she'll do with it - or not bother? Does she tell him?

J explains <u>need</u> to invest - to make money work, make jobs for people

7. Rose has been thinking. The prospect of easy money has entranced her. She comes into the morning room (looking for Georgina? Virginia?) Sunday morning feeling. They (somehow) get talking about money. Rose's money. Her dreams. He gets the gist. A secret deal is arranged. He will act as her broker. She will sign the necessary papers which will place her money in his hands to invest. Rose thrilled with private visions of wealth. The deed will soon be done.

They are really asking him the question. How much

8. It's a few days later. The panatrope is being delivered, placed, //~~and played.~~// Disturbing letter from America, he goes out.

is he affected? He
might be rather
evasive.

9. The news of the crash, through Richard and Georgina. They wonder exactly how James will be
affected. He comes in, //is told and stunned by
the news.// (or he already knows?)

Does R. go to see J?

10. Rose innocent of her impending doom, is informed by Hudson of the Wall St. crash. They
say, poor James, it's lucky you weren't tempted,
Rose. Rose has an unexpected summons from
James, to see him in his room. The downstairs
are puzzled.

11. James, agitated, tells Rose what has happened.
Very subdued. Rose says she doesn't care, bravely.
James grateful for her forbearance. James relieved but ashamed, as Rose leaves the room
quietly.

Glad she's taken it so well.

End on Rose.

END OF ACT ONE

ACT TWO

1. Rose is acting very strangely downstairs. Finally,
Hudson extracts a confession. He is stunned. Learns
                                    must keep it to herself
also that nobody else knows. Feels //it is his duty
to inform his Lordship.// They may be questioned
by Mrs. B. But what else can he do? Hudson feels
Rose has been very foolish, which sends her out
in a flood of tears.

//Or, H. asks R. to
inform Her Ladyship.
She refuses. Then
he must.//

Hudson—sympathy and rebuke

V., who has heard from Rose, innocently tells R. about it. He explodes!

2. Hudson has just informed R. and V. of what has happened. Richard conceals his anger from Hudson, then vents it on V. (briefly) Where is James? Visiting financial advisers? He has need of it.

3. James returns and is told by H. that R. wishes to see him. James somewhat puzzled and annoyed, goes into the M.R.—and faces his father. V. embarrassed, has to leave. The row begins. The house becomes aware of it. Luncheon is postponed. Even cancelled. Now perhaps H. attempts sympathy with R., is savagely rebuffed. She goes out.

4. //~~Downstairs' anxiety about whereabouts of R. Not seen since morning.~~// H. angry with her behavior. Mrs. B sympathetic. V., anxious about her, calling her, possibly—

5. eating alone with G., as the girls wait for the outcome. The strange disrupting row which has rent the whole house.

6. The row continues unabated and all the home truths come out. James feels at first that he is being treated unreasonably. "She is a free agent. She came to me on her own accord."
   <u>R.</u>   She is under our care and protection.

   Hudson has to report that Rose has gone missing—to V. who needed her for an afternoon engagement.
The act must end with James leaving his father. It has all been said. Both are exhausted, spent. James goes to his room, claiming to have been sent there like a naughty boy.

Or maybe he too storms out.
                    (They think R. has gone to her

(room, find out later she's out.

?   (And they don't see J. return to

(his room.

Where has he been? Anywhere interesting? His club—can't face his friends. Who knows? Nowhere to go.

Maybe end on James. The panatrope has arrived. He puts on a record. Sits and broods. Or, buoyant jazz. Ironic.

ACT III
It is later in the day.

1. Richard's anger is abated, put into perspective by V. G. attempts to see James, fails to be allowed in. Hears his gramophone. Richard cannot bring himself to make the peace. "Leave him there," he declares and goes out.

R. still angry. Ashamed. Calmed by V. "Damned nerve— seemed to blame <u>me</u> for his shortcomings."

2. Growing anxiety and annoyance with R., downstairs. H's feelings of guilt, did he do the right thing? "Unlike Rose" anxieties.

Mary saw her go out.

3. Silent dinner which J. fails to appear at.

G. wants to know what was said and why.

4. G. leaves to seek out J. She is admitted. He seems low and excitable in turns. And then scene develops. The crucial one. In which she tries to lift him, make light of it. "I have no friends," he says. "Nowhere to go." "Everything I do I seem to make a mess of." She accuses him of self-pity. Is alternatively angry with him and sorry for him. He is much loved, he has so much to offer. What's the matter with him? He feels she treats him like a sick lap dog. Nursing him. Slowly he turns his appeal, centers his hopes on her. She's the only one who can save him. Of course she loves him,

On the Richard scene "as my father told me" ask him.

she's always loved him. But like a dear brother.
A precious brother. She leaves him thinking she
has revived him. He's hungry. She'll have something sent up. <u>Mary</u>.

5. It's now 8:30. Rose hasn't turned up for supper.
Concern continues. Should the police be alerted?
Edw. and Daisy speculate (but not about her death,
nobody thinks of that. At night. This may be the
flaw in the Rose thing—Edw. and D. <u>would</u> speculate and then I'm screwed, aren't I. It must be
tried, perhaps. Jumped in the river. Briefly men-
tioned by Edw., stomped on by others.

"All jumping off
building" The paper

?

6. James alone in his room, is examining the con-
tents of his life. The war mementoes. The letters
and papers. His will? The money has gone—it's
just the house—which of course his father and
V. must have. He must cause the least possible
fuss.

No-perhaps-instead-

*Second Narrative Exposition

Somehow it might be possible that early on, in his
high period, he announces he wants to reorganize his
life. Sort out the jumble of his affairs. Redecorate
the room. Retain only what is necessary. America
has given him this need to unclutter himself of the
past. That has been the problem. Backward thinking.
A kind of sentimental attachment to unimportant
things. A hanging onto past traditions. Irrelevancies.
He has said all this to G. She is delighted. She will
help him redecorate. Take out the fustiness. Expunge
the memories of the war. The mementoes. She doesn't
see that he has nothing to replace it with. The fra-
gility of his condition. The scene with his father is
in a sense what he wants. Ironically, to admit to the
mistakes, freely. Tear them up like the letters. De-

stroy them like the war mementoes. "Why does one
keep these things?" to G. "Do you keep mementoes
of the war? No, she declares. Why must a man? Even
his medal. Well, for state occasions perhaps. He says
of his room, this is the only room in the house that
hasn't been changed since V.

He starts the sort-out.
Everything is out of
the drawers in piles.
But he can't get rid of
anything. M. sees a
photo of him in
uniform, admires it -
puts it down & we
find it again, as she
left it - when
Richard. . . .

So that we are misled. Mary comes in and says "Having a clear out?" Yes, he says. And she helps and
they flirt and she mentions his mother . . .

Whom he can't expunge. Nor Hazel. Nor the war
mementoes. Nor the letters. Nothing can he get rid
of. They are all him. And must be left as a memory
of him. He is locked irrevocably in his forlorn past.
And Richard is left at the end to gaze across at them.
The only and painful memorial.

So he has made his decision and is calm. Ordered.
The normal self to the outside world. He eats the
meal. The simple last supper. He packs a bag. He
is going to see a man about his financial situation.
Stay the night away with a friend.

He comes out of the room. Meets Daisy who tells
him Georgina is writing a letter in her room. "Don't
disturb her." He comes downstairs. Looks in at the
M.R. and is caught by Virginia. "Where's father?"
In the bath. "Do you want to see him?" Please see
him. Please make it up. She starts to try to explain
—but he's not listening. Need a bit of time. I'm
going away for the weekend. Back when? Sunday
night (firmly). Got a lot of things to sort out.
Salvage (financial matters, she thinks.)

Meets Hudson in the hall. It's a cold night. You'll
need your coat sir. And an afterthought from James.
How's Rose? And Hudson lies. James, unaware of

her absence, says (she took it remarkably well, the news) Or maybe he doesn't even need to say this. It's unspoken between them. As James goes, Georgina comes downstairs. Just missing him. A jarring note. Her surprise that he's going to visit a friend without telling her.

Downstairs 11:00 P.M. Mrs. B. refuses to go to bed till Rose returns. Hudson is worried. Undecided. Won't lock up. Will leave the back door open for her. What friends has she got to go to? She hasn't got any friends. Ironic echo.

Then at midnight. Banging. Policemen at the door. Hudson wakes, answers the door. Mrs. B. wakes. They think it's news about Rose, in trouble.

Policemen, tight-lipped, ask to see his Lordship. They're summoned. We see them come down. Richard is his new silk dressing gown. And the news is broken. And the letter is handed over. The policemen retire.

H., hovering in the hall

V., shattered, weeps. R., stiff upper lip. Says,
                              Hudson
you. . .inform. . . //the servants.// Leaves.

She watches him stumble (with the letter)—then rings for Hudson. He arrives and goes into the M.R. with her.

We don't need to see what happens.

Start on Mrs. B hearing her.

Rose comes in downstairs. Mrs. B. overcome with relief. Reconciliation and forgiveness. R. càlm. Went on a bus ride, that's all. To Ilford. Wanted to remember Gregory, that's all. No harm in that. Feel better. Then H. appears in the doorway. Ashen-faced.

Richard, alone in James' room. The fire out. The photos of the dead all around him. Memories. The letter in his hands and possible James' simple statement. Richard crying. End of photo of James.

So, absent reactions are Georgina, the servants—we only hear the news once. To Richard and Virginia—this is probably right.

FIRST BASH
"All the King's Horses"
October
*Act 1, Scenes 1, 2, 3 & 4

1.   INT. HALL & STAIRS. DAY Empty hall. Front doors open. Edward brings in a heavy trunk. Leaves it, goes out again. After a moment James enters. Jazzy American clothes. Bow tie. He stands, surveying the emptiness. Readjusting himself to the familiar surroundings. M.R. door opens. Mary comes out with pan and brush. James turns. Mary blushes, smiles.

J. Hello, who are you?
M. Mary, sir.
J. How long have you been here? (M. panics, tries to count.) You don't have to be exact.
M. About six weeks now, sir.
J. (grins) You know who I am do you?
M. (beams) Oh, yes, sir...(Hudson comes down the stairs)
H. Welcome home, sir. I'm sorry I wasn't down to meet you myself.

Dissappointment at absence of family

J. Hello, Hudson. (H. helps him off with the coat--slightly starts at the suit and "look" of James.) (Hands it to Mary to hang up.)
H. Did you have a //~~good~~// pleasant voyage, sir?
J. //~~It was all right.~~// Yes, I suppose so. Plenty of activity on board. But I don't care for the ocean much.

H. You're looking extremely fit, if I may say so, sir.

J. Thank you. Yes, I'm feeling//~~quite~~//well. All well here?
   (above "quite": very)

H. Oh, yes, sir. Everything much the same as usual.

J. That plant's new.

H. A gift to his Lordship from the French ambassador, sir.

J. From French equatorial Africa, by the look of it. Is my father in?

H. His Lordship and Lady Bellamy are visiting Madame Tussaud's this afternoon, sir—an official reception for its reopening. They send their regrets for not being here to welcome you, but they will be back in time for dinner.

J. Miss Georgina?

H. Miss Georgina has been visiting some friends of her fiance, the Marquis of Stockbridge, sir, but she has promised to be back in time for dinner also. (H. starts to lift heavy cases.)

Edw. It's all right, Mr. Hudson, I'll carry them. (Hudson puts them down in some relief.)

H. Is there anything I can get you, sir?

J. No, thanks--I think I'll have a bath//~~and a rest.~~ //(He leads the way.)

H. Mary--run a bath for the major.

M. Yes, sir. (She hurries upstairs.) (J. watches her go.)

H. The new housemaid. sir. Quite willing and dependable. (James grunts his approval and follows her upstairs.)

2. <u>INT. M.R.   NIGHT</u>
Richard and Virginia and James. (Dressed for dinner.) Relaxed with drinks. James placing an emerald necklace round her neck. She is dazzled.

V. (ecstatic) Richard--look--Oh, James darling, it's beautiful. You shouldn't have...oh thank you so much. (She kisses him.)

J. (pleased) Now father's turn. (Hands him a box.)

R. My dear boy——you've gone much too far.

J. Nonsense,//I've missed//Christmas --and all

I was in Arizona last & heaven knows where for

birthdays for the past year. //Least I could do.//

Making up for it.

(R. brings out silk dressing gown.)

V. Oh put it on...put it on.

R. I will (He does.)

J. Does it fit?

Much more fuss from J.

R. Perfectly. (He parades.)   School-boy excitement.

V. It matches his eyes. It's always been my favorite colour for him. You are clever, James.

J. That's for Georgina--(points to third box.)

R. I feel amazing. Amazing in it. Delightful. Thank you, old boy. You've spent a fortune on us.

J. Well, without wishing to boast, father, I can afford it at the moment. (R. and V. stare at each other) Time for that later. (pours himself another drink) How was Madame Tussaud's?

R. Far too life-like. People one once knew personally staring quizzically at one. I dislike it intensely.

in wax

V. He enjoyed it immensely. Will you forgive me, darlings--I'm going to change my dress. I know exactly the one for this. I'll be back in two seconds. (She goes.)

R. I doubt that. (p. they smile at each other, settle on the enjoyment of seeing each other after so long an absence.)

R. It is good to have you home. (pats his shoulder) We've missed you, all of us, in our different ways, including the servants.

J. (smiles) What's been happening.

Didn't you get any

R. (laughs) You did get some of our letters, I hope?

they seldom tell you much in my experience. Either

J. Yes, ~~but//I've never believed much in letters. Ei-~~
full of reassuring noises
~~ther//~~ dashed off in haste--or//~~they contain bro-
mides, half-truths//~~on the grounds that the reader
is too far away to act, if needed.//~~They seldom
speak the truth in my experience.//~~

R. //~~You may be right~~.//(smiles)

J. What are you doing these days?

Much less of all this.
More jagged.

R. Well, the government fell in May--by pursuing
the wrong tactics--not that we realized that at
the time. Ramsey Macdonald is as much of a
nonentity as before. Baldwin is sleepy and un-
inspiring in opposition. There are rumours of
of leaders
change... I've been kept pretty busy. Weekly
meetings of the League of Nations. A lot of talking, little else. Marking time, really. Waiting
for something to happen. Quite a happy time,
though. Time for the family--travel. I'm rather
content at the moment.

But you don't want
to hear about that.

J - I want to hear
about you.

J. What about Georgina and her Marquis? Is that
a good thing?

R. He's a delightful fellow, I'm very fond of him.
There's been some resistance from his family, but
you know about that.

J. //~~Yes. How's she bearing up to this separation
business//~~
//~~Rather//~~   //~~to our surprise//~~

R. //~~Amazingly well.//~~ //~~She's calmed down a good
deal.//~~

J. But it's not a good idea, is it, separating people.
Rather an outmoded and silly custom, I've always felt. It seldom achieves its purpose--it
strengthens the romantic and fantasy part of it
all. And loses the reality. If they survive, they
come together with a hopelessly false picture of
each other.

R. Yes, I think you may be right, but try telling
that to Lord Stockbridge. (J. smiles, drinks) What

about you now? America seems to have suited you--from what you've said in your letters. Do you mean to go and live there permanently?

Too soon
G - will you go back?
That's what we want
to
know

J. I don't know. I've been thinking hard about it. The impact of the people..the life, on one, was amazing. It knocked me sideways. Their outlook is so extraordinarily different. Maybe if one got used to it, it might become less attractive. I still have so many ties here. If I can see them now--in the fresh light that America's given me, maybe I'll have gained from it all I need.

R. Well, that's encouraging--we don't want to lose you for good.

(G. bursts in)

G. Jumbo...(hugs, kisses) Darling Jumbo. More attractive than ever.

J. Same to you.

G. Oh no--I'm all hot and flustered--driving like mad to get back to see you. I must change. Oh...we've missed you horribly, haven't we, Uncle Richard? We've been miserable. Don't go away for so long again.

J. You won't need me for long--if all I hear is true.

G. feels his "almost" resentment. End on that jagged note

G. Oh...yes....

J. Congratulations. (kisses her)

G. Thank you (She feels awkward--he saves it)

J. Present for you. (hands her box)

G. Jumbo..what is it? (opens it, sable fur) Oh../ heavens..it's sable..oh (she puts it on, parades) kisses him)

J. I hope your fiance will take it in the right spirit!

R. Virginia has a necklace, and I have this (parades) (Hudson enters)

H. (amazed) (though with discretion) Dinner is served, my lord.

A touch more about Eliz., her home and prohibition

3. <u>INT. DINING ROOM   NIGHT</u>
After dinner. Coffee and brandy and liqueurs.

Relaxed atmosphere. James animated. The others caught up in his mood.

J. Excellent. Tell Mrs. Bridges, will you, Hudson?

H. She'll be most pleased to hear it, sir.

J. Elizabeth has just acquired an English cook--but she's not a patch on Mrs. B.

R. Tell us about Elizabeth. How is she?

J. She's in her element. Practically the most favored young hostess in New York. Her house is full of people--writers, politicians, famous aviators. God knows what-all talking about money. The lions of the moment are brokers.

V. Is that all they talk about?

J. Yes.

G. How boring.

J. Not if you're making it. And everybody is.

R. Including you.

J. Including me, father. Thanks to Elizabeth's husband. He was a partner in Goldman, Sachs--the big trading corporation. Spending a day with him in Wall St. was one of the most fascinating experiences of my life.

G. Tell us how much you've made!

J. You see—you are interested. Enough to sell this place and buy somewhere bigger.

V. We don't want anywhere bigger, do we darling?

R. Somewhere smaller if anything.

J. All right. We'll keep this--and buy somewhere in France. Or a yacht. Do you want a yacht?

R. Are you serious?

J. Absolutely serious, father. I'm invested up to the hilt and making profits every day. Not just me. Everyone has their ears open for tips--waiters, window cleaners, chauffeurs, nurses. (Shot of Daisy and Hudson)

V. Is it healthy?

(J. Why not? These are prosperous times. Isn't it
(what we've all been struggling towards since the

war? For Heaven's sake, don't let's be ashamed
of it now we got it.

G. <u>We</u> haven't got it—have we?

J. We will have. If we want it.

Risk. Uncertainty.
Frightened at first.

V. I find it rather unsettling.

R. Hedonistic!

A rambling, jagged
speech of personal
impressions.

J. If you mean by that—living life to the full and
not missing opportunities, I agree, it is hedonistic. But is that wrong, father?

G. //<s>Surely it can't last, can it? I mean</s>// But not everyone
can be rich, can they. There's not enough.

J. They're making enough--more than enough,
Georgina, that's the point. Maybe I'm making
it sound cold and calculating; it isn't the true
feeling. These's magic in the air. That's how it
hits the outsider, anyway.

R. But you're not the outsider--you've been sucked
in.

V. Wasn't there a man over here, a few weeks ago,
whose empire came tumbling down?

R. Clarence Hatry

J. I read about it. He was a crook, wasn't he?

R. Even so, there are cautionary notes of warning
over here, James.

J. There've been rumours all year. It's part of the
game. Nothing to worry about. I offer you a
toast to our future prosperity. (He smiles at
them--they smile a little nervously back.)

H & Mary (& Daisy?)
private moment with
Spotted Dick.

4.   <u>INT. S.H.   NIGHT</u>
Late evening. Cocoa after the dinner is cleared
and finished. Daisy and Edw.--Rose and

Start with Mrs. B.

Mrs. B--(Mary) and Hudson. Rather high,
but tired.

Edw. Millionaire chauffeurs--that'll be the day.

D. It's true, Eddy. They listen in to conversations in the back of men's motors--and go

Later   (and put their savings on, don't they, Mr.
            (Hudson?

            (

H. It all smacks of gambling to me, Daisy--
and you know my views on that subject.

D. But it isn't gambling, Mr. Hudson, because
nobody loses; that's what the Major says.
It's called--what is it?

H. Speculating. Another word for the same
thing, if you look in the dictionary.

Edw. And it's no good for us, Daisy. We haven't
got any savings to speculate with.

D. No, but Rose has. (As Rose comes in)

R. You seen all the presents he's come back
with? Her Ladyship's necklace is the most
beautiful thing I've ever seen.

D. I'd rather have Miss Georgina's fur.

R. Wonder how rich he is.

H. It's all on paper, Rose. And I question the
morality of it--making money without
working for it. It's against all my beliefs.

Edw. But if it can do some good, Mr. Hudson.
Better than having it sitting at the Post
Office, isn't it--like Rose's nest egg?

D. Yeh, if I were you, Rose, I'd invest it.

R. How?

D. Well, ask the Major. He'd do it for you.

R. I couldn't do that.

D. I would.

R. Yeh, well, I'm not you, Daisy. I agree with
Mr. Hudson. Don't seem right, that's why.

Edw. You have a flutter on the horses sometimes.
      (Mary and Mrs. B. come in)

Mrs. B. Not a scrap left on his plate--for any of the
courses. Does my heart good. Mind if I have
my chair, Daisy, please.

D. Sorry, Mrs. B. (She gets up--Mrs. B. settles)

Mrs. B. Have you got my cocoa, Mary?

Mary Here you are, Mrs. Bridges.

Edw. What do you think of the Major, then, Mary, eh?

Mary. He's good lookin, isn't he?

D. And rich.

Mrs. B. How rich is he?

H. Nobody knows, Mrs. Bridges, and I think we should leave the subject, if you don't mind. It's not doing some of the younger members of the staff any good at all. (pointed look at Edw. and Daisy.) (But Rose, thoughtful)

So far it won't do. (but it doesn't matter)

The key to James is volatility--mistakenly put down to the American influence--in fact, a reading of his own condition.

The clue is that he is just slightly <u>over</u>-reacts to every situation. The first stirrings of manic-depressive state. R. and V. think (if they have the short scene together) James is volatile America.

Just the slightest unease throughout. Short jagged scenes. No quite settling on subjects. <u>R.</u>--Hard to keep his mind on any <u>one</u> subject. <u>V.</u>--So much to tell. (reassuring). She may also say--America's given him zip. So much energy; now we must help him channel it.

J. constantly changing the subject. the household constantly thrown slightly out of its stride, having to make quick readjustments.

*ACT I   LIST OF SCENES

1. Arrival
2. Presents
3. Spotted Dick

4. Dinner
5. Downstairs, money. Rose.
6. Goodnights. J. off to bed. R. and V.
7. James and Hudson—pajamas and cigars. Then ghosts—and Georgina.
8. Morning. Mary and breakfast
9. James, alone again. Rose

> (and maybe the act ends here, on Rose secretly pleased.)

Act I—too long. Must be condensed further!

*SECOND PLOTTING   ACTS II & III
Act II

1. Panatrope installed. J. happy. G. ready to go out and choose wallpaper and curtains. . . Mary brings in disturbing letter. Change of plans. G. left standing.

2. //~~Hall. J. rushing out. Black Thursday. Richard tries to stop him, holding newspaper. Not now, father.~~//

3.&6. Rose, happy, on her own. Hudson comes in with disturbing news of Black Thursday. Rose doesn't let on. Rose pale.

<small>Black Thursday. Rose doesn't let on. Rose pale.</small>

(//4. ~~J. defends crisis. R. anxious. J. the bankers will step in. Edgy throughout.~~//

4. Rose, along corridor. You wanted to see me? James carries scene. He tells her. She seems to take it well.

Put in after 3 & 6   6. H. complacently tells the company of Wall Street crash. "Told you so" feeling. Rose goes pale. Maybe unexpectedly breaks down. Horrified incredulity.

5. Downstairs—Rose has confessed. H. incredulous. Gentleman bit. Don't tell anyone. (as Edw. and D. come in)

6. Richard worried for J. Where is he? Out. V. then

drops bombshell about Rose. Must do something. J. arrives back and all is lost.

1. J. panatrope. G. brings in letter from U.S. Bad news. J. leaves her standing, goes quickly out.
2. Rose happy. H. comes in with Black Thursday news. Worried about the Major. Rose pales.
3. Rose visits James (who was on the point of calling for her anyway). Explains what it means. Can't pull out. Bankers will step in. Question of confidence. But she susses out, things don't look very good, Then makes a brave show of it. J. somehow relieved by her understanding.

Friday

4. R. pale and hesitant, "confesses" to H. and Mrs. H. furious. Told you so. Mrs. B. sympathetic. H.—Don't tell anyone. Keep it to yourself. (as Edw. and D. enter)

Wed. Lunchtime

5. Richard (and G.) and V. And we learn that Wall Street crashed. J. has been out a lot, keeping things to himself. Trying to arrange things. Then comes bombshell from V.—Rose has told her privately. Richard furious. J. returns. V. and G. scatter—or go to lunch which is ready and announced by H.
6. R. and J. in essence. Raised voices, tensions.
7. The silent luncheon. Just the girls. H. asked to summon them (?) Or V. stops him from going.
8. The return to the Big Scene. The home truths which are told—followed by exhaustion. J. goes out.
9. Girls hear the door shut. Get up. V. into R. But we follow G. upstairs. Knock on door. No answer. Music heard.

Act III

1. Rose defending her action (telling V.) to H. Rose's collapse. Not the money. It's Gregory. Freedom. Trapped here now <u>forever</u>! She storms out.

Act 2? (
      (
      (
      (
      (

H. Furious—she always uses that argument. Why didn't she leave when she had the money? Mrs. B. (soothing him) She doesn't mean it. It's made her think about Gregory. That's all.

2. R. and V. R. eating heartily from a tray. Still angry. Playing jazz, up in his room—let him stay there, feeling. G. worried. V. soothes R. down.

Goes into Act II

3. G. decides to jolly him out of it. We hear her outside insisting on entrance. James acquiesces. She comes in. She cajoles him back to life (she thinks). She offers love (her sort). Hope. She gets angry and exasperated. She finally springs into action. The new life—come on, clear it all out. Finds her own letters. Exclaims. But James is dead by now. Tomorrow we start in earnest, and I'll ask for some tea to be sent up to you. She goes.

4. V. asks H. where Rose is. Rose has missed an appointment. Rose went out, my lady. Brief exchange. H. expresses his regrets. In some way blames himself. There was a lot of excitement when the Major returned, talk of money. It went to Rose's head, I'm afraid. V.—Yes. Well, tell her I want to see her about my (something) when she returns. Will you?

This is important (
      (
      (
      (
      (

5. James, busy, sorting etc. Calm, slow. ordered. Mary scene. Flirts, Packing, etc. Burn all letters. He Leaves her. At work. Comes into the passage. Knocks on G.'s door. Just finishing a letter, she says. With you in a minute. He walks on.

6. Downstairs. Looks in at V. Where's father? Having a bath. Cooling off, James! I'm so sorry. He didn't mean half of what he said. He's told me. He is ashamed. He wants to apologize.

V. //~~Are you going away—out?~~//

J. Yes. (vaguely, looking at room) Won't be in for dinner. Going away for a few days. Sort things out.

V. Yes. Perhaps that's best.

Hall. Hudson. Coat. Possible mention of Rose. H. lies as James goes. Door closes. G. comes down with letter. Surprised.

7. Late. Mrs. B.—Where is the girl? Won't go to bed until she returns. Won't lock up. Scare. She's got no friends to go to. Front door.
8. H. opens to cops. Who ask to see Lord B. etc. "They're in bed." H. shows them into M.R. H. hurries upstairs.
9. Cops—wait, look around. Impassive. R. and V. come down in dressing gowns. The news is broken. The letter handed over. Shock and dismay. They leave. H., looking anxious, looks through open door at distress.
10. Mrs. B., downstairs, overjoyed at Rose's return. Where've you bin? On a bus. All right now. Sorry. Calm. Then ashen H. appears.
11. Richard alone in James's room.

Dear Father—You mustn't reproach yourself for what I'm doing. You only told me some truths I've known about myself for a long time. //~~The war should have finished me off.~~// Do you remember me telling you about that German officer in the shell crater at Passchendaele—the one who could have finished me, but declined to—well, I'm doing the job that should have been done then. Try to see it as a dignified action—an officer's way out when he can no longer do justice to himself or the men under his command. I have come here so that I wouldn't make a mess of my room or disturb the servants more than necessary.

Give my last fond love to Virginia—and to Georgina.

Goodbye, father, Forgive me.

*SECOND TRY—DINNER SCENE, ACT I

Scene 4. Dinner.

J. Scared. Eliz's social life hectic. Talked about hostess. Kind of people. Brokers. Money, excitement.

Pudding—no room *This pudding becomes the portentous Spotted Dick.

I didn't like the place at all to begin with—unnerved by it. //~~The winter (month?) spent with~~ That first winter with E. ~~Eliz—heaven help anyone.~~ That time spent with// A quiet evening at home, by her standards, means no less than 15 people to dinner.

R. But she gave you the introductions.

J. Yes, it paid off, I suppose—and when I got back to N.Y. I was adjusted and began to enjoy myself.

G. Is she happy with that awful smooth husband of hers?

J. Dana—yes, they seem all right, whenever they bump into each other. She's in her element, fast becoming the most talked-about young hostess in town. House is packed with politicians, writers, and society ladies—but the real lions of the moment are the brokers. The talk's all money.

V. How boring.

J. //~~You don't understand~~// No—it's extraordinary. The excitement—uncertainty—like a game. Dana took me to Wall St. one day. Incredible experience. Feeling of fellowship—rather like the war.

//~~R~~//

V. Dana advised you on money matters, did he?

J. Yes—he's just become a partner in Goldman Sachs big trading corporation. Right in the thick of it all. I owe all my new-found wealth to his expertise.

G. Jumbo, how rich are you?

Is this Chateau Lafite?
R. Yes.
J. Marvellous. Haven't tasted anything like it in 2 years.
V. Prohibition is the maddest of all laws.
G. Don't the smart people break it all the time?
J. Everyone breaks it and fights over it. Eliz & Dana keep their cellar in a specially built gazebo.
R. Is she happy with that husband of hers?
J.//~~Ecstatically~~// In her element. Most talked about hostess in town, house jammed with politicians, writers, the best society. . .

J. Not a millionaire, but rich enough to give you any wedding you ask for. . . . .the best trousseau, etc.

*FIRST TRY - THE ROW
Richard and James

J. Look—she came and asked me, Father, of her own free will. What was I supposed to do—turn her away?

R. Well, of course you should have. Have you no sense? It's an unshakeable rule—one never meddles with a servant's money.

Tighten this page
Come on!

Some law that only gentlemen make money.

J. I did <u>not</u> meddle with it, father. I invested it. Soundly. (R., harsh laugh). <u>I</u> couldn't know what
       had a talk
would happen. Anyway, I've discussed it with her. She took it very well.

R. You must have been very persuasive.

J. I didn't have to be. She's intelligent—she knew
      knew
it wasn't my fault //at once.// She took the risk.

She's not some halfwit, father. Some old ga-ga- family retainer. She's a bright, independent girl.

R. How did she? //Know what the risk was?// Did you tell her or did you say it was all easy—//and did she put herself in your hands, James?// Trust you, James, as she's always trusted us.

J. Look—it's not some sort of exclusive club, father, only for gentlemen to become rich. You're out of date!

R. If she had become rich, what then? How would a girl like Rose know what to do with wealth? You'd have given her ideas and dreams and responsibilities she could never have dealt with. Either way you'd have ruined her life.

J. What arrogance—to assume <u>we</u> know what she'd have done. My God! //(Exclusive club)//

R. //We know because// she's spent all her life with

us, under our care and protection. Now what's
to become of her? She has nothing—and we can't
afford to pay her back.

Not at the moment.

J. Yes, all right, father. But I will try. //~~and honour
the debt.~~//

R. You? You're wiped out, James. //~~How can you~~?/
/ Ruined. Face the facts, boy. //~~You're ruined~~//
—and you've ruined her. I'm only glad your mother
was spared this.

J. Mother?

R. Yes, //~~what would she have said~~//—My God, she
wouldn't have believed it of you, James. It would
have broken her heart to see what you have done.

J. (shaky) Mother—lived in a different time. We've
moved on. We've fought a war.

R. Don't use the war as an excuse. The war's got
nothing to do with this.

J. Hasn't it?

keep

R. We fought the war to preserve the world your
mother knew. To preserve decent standards of
civilized behavior.

J, Now you're talking like an old fool.

R. What?

J. You honestly believe. . .

R. How dare you.

J. Hopeless even trying. . .

R. Hopeless-yes-hopeless, James, that's the word for
it—exactly.

J. What do you mean?

R. I mean you, boy—everything you do—everything you turn to—seems to come to nothing.
Why? Can you tell me? Why—with all your
end
advantages, does it always turn out the same?

J. Explain yourself, father. Come—let's have this
out—once and for all!

R. So much you could have done with your life. So
much to offer, in whatever field you'd chose—
that bye-election you fought—now there was
something—//~~if you hadn't just folded up after~~
~~one setback.~~// [you should've stuck with it] You had a flair for politics, you
could've

Virginia's agreed to help—we'll make it up. You
could sell the house if necessary.

J. Rose is my problem, father. Not yours.

R. Ours, James. Ours together. //~~Believe me, I never~~ [What are we doing, talking like this?]
~~meant us to talk like this.~~// I simply want to
understand and help. (Believe me.)

J. Help—you accuse me of some kind of immoral
act with Rose. You attack my character on all
fronts—help—you haven't begun to understand—! I know what I am. I don't need you to
tell me. //~~I'm perfectly aware that since the war~~
~~I've been nothing more than some kind of~~
~~onlooker—I've lost a wife—I've lost my money~~
~~—though that's the least of it. . . .~~//

Richard isn't quite right. That's the problem.

R. James, my dear boy. . .

J. No—<u>no</u>, Father—no conciliations <u>please</u>. I couldn't
stand that. That's how we always end up, patching
the wounds—let's leave them open this time. //
~~Let the air get at them—let nature heal if it~~
~~must~~—//agree to part—<u>honestly</u>—for once (He
storms out.)

(Georgina, in hall)

G. Jumbo—(upstairs)

R. Let him go, Georgina.

G. No—what have you said to him? Jumbo—(she
follows, V. comes out, to R. R. storms back)

V. Richard—//~~what's happened between you?~~//
(G. to outside door. It's locked.)

G. Jumbo—it's Georgina—let me in, please Jumbo. (sound of music. Defiant jazz).

Bleak.

*AMENDED LIST OF SCENES
ACT I

1. James's return. Hall. Mary and Hudson.
2. Presents. James and Richard and Virginia and Georgina.
3. Servants hall. Reactions and excitement.
4. Dinner. America. The Glory of money.
5. Reflected downstairs. Hudson explains the market. Rose.
6. J. and H. (cigar). Then J. alone, ghosts. G. warmth and mutual comfort.
7. J. and Mary, next morning. Annoyance.
8. J., bored, finds new outlet for energy with Rose.

ACT II

9. Old and new. J's room. Panatrope—dead soldier. Edw. as magpie. Letter from U.S.
10. Hudson. Prophet of doom. Wall St. crash. Rose hears.
11. J. avoids Rose.
12. Walks into reception of R., V., G. Owns up. Their incredulity. His grit.
13. R. finds him. He breaks news. She seems to take it well. He's relieved.
14. R's breakdown, below. H's remedies. Rejected by Rose.
15. Richard learns from V. what J's done. Orders him. Consternation of house.
16. J. and Richard. The Rose affair. J. defends. Open row develops.
17. Awful girls' lunch. H. sent to see what's what.

18. H. kept out—sees defiant Rose leave house by front door.
19. J's life laid bare. Unfortunate things said. .R. belatedly patches, J. rejects.
20. Hall. J. to room. G. follows. R. to Morning room. V. follows.
21. G. bangs on locked door. Then hears music on panatrope.

ACT III

22. Downstairs—reactions to absent Rose.
23. R and V—his anger, her attempts to pacify. H's justifications re: Rose, accepted.
24. G's second attempt to see J.—grimly packing up. The love scene. J. finally rejected.
25. Mrs. B. waits for R. Mary says J's asked for tea.
26. M. and J. echoes of Sarah. Departure.
27. No answer from G.
28. J. into Morning room. V.—Richard in bath. Goodbye's. J. calm.
29. J. and H.—farewells.
30. H. and Mrs. B.—anxious about R. Doorbell.
31. Hudson meets the cops.
32. Rose returns—Mrs. B.
33. Cops break news to R and V.
34. Rose's explanation to Mrs. B. Hudson's ashen face.
35. Richard alone in dead son's room.

Act III, Scene 24

G. into room. Door unlocked. Doesn't see J. for a moment. Kneeling behind desk. Packing trunk. His mind is pretty well made up. She's frightened—premonition. He comes to realize she's last desperate lifeline.

G. Jumbo? (no answer) (sees him) (comes to him) What are you doing?

J. What we planned. Clearing stuff out. You come to help? (not looking at her, dumps mortar shell into trunk)

G. (hesitates) Yes. (kneels beside him) Where are you taking it all to—a war museum?

J. Rag and bone cart.

G. (picks up shell) What's this?

J. German mortar shell. (takes it, puts it back) Good for scrap.

G. (picks up German watch) Shouldn't this. .have gone back to some man's widow?

J. Whose widow? I found it in the mud. Fair game. Spoils of war. Didn't you keep //anything// souvenirs? (she shakes her head) (He gets up, opens cupboard, throws in boots, uniform, tearing them off the pegs) (She gets up, wanders to desk—sees photos, letters and papers)

G. Jumbo—what happened between you and Uncle Richard? (no answer) //Was it about Rose? Tell me.// (She turns on him.)

J. Doesn't matter.
     If it was about Rose.

G. It does. It was unfair of him to blame you. It wasn't your fault. //He upset you, didn't he?// (no answer) Don't keep it all bottled up. Tell me, _please_. (He stares at her, she's got his attention now.)

J. (helpless) //I can't. Ask him about it. It's public knowledge, anyway.// But one thing I won't forgive him for. //No use.// Using Mother against
     //realize//
me. Didn't he know? Coming back on that damned boat. //All that ocean.// Staring out at all that damned ocean. Knowing she was somewhere. //I wanted to know the exact spot. Just mark it— do you understand?//

G. (horrified) Oh yes, I do. Yes. Oh, poor Jumbo.

J. And he used her money—as a _weapon_ //against me.//

G. (hugs him) He didn't mean it—Jumbo, you
mustn't hold it against him. You must think of
the future—that's what you said. Please don't
look back. (J. relaxes, picks up a photo)

J. (smiles) Photo of you and Hazel. Want it? (she
relaxes)

G. Don't you? There are lots of photos here—you
ought to put them in a scrapbook. (nervous
laugh—which he cuts)

J. Who for?

G. The family. Our children. . .

J. Your children. Not mine.

G. Oh, Jumbo, don't be bitter and unhappy. Please.
~~I can't bear it. I know //you've lost all that~~ things are difficult
~~money—it's awful~~ //—but please. . .

J. The money's nothing. I've only one regret about
the money. I can't give you the wedding I promised.

G. That doesn't matter.

J. It matters to me!

G. You'll still <u>be</u> there—you'll be the most important person, you know that. You'll be my support.

J. Your husband will be your support. What are you
talking about? I'll be of no use whatever. (He
deliberately picks up her bundle of letters.)

G. //~~You'll always be dear to me, my dearest friend~~
~~in the world.~~// But I love <u>him</u>. He //~~depends on~~/ needs
/ me more than you do. //~~We've gone our own~~
~~way for too long.~~// What happened between us
was over—long ago. We've gone our own ways. . .

J. But just now. . . .

G. //~~A trick of memory, that's all it was you know~~
~~it was. Please, I must go—I've got to write my~~
~~letter to him. He's miserable when they don't~~
~~arrive. You'll always be dear to me. My dearest~~
~~friend in the world. (Kiss. Goes.)~~//

G. It was nothing. A trick of memory. You know it was. Please. Let me go. I've got to write my letter to him. He's miserable when they don't arrive. (comes to kiss him) You'll always be dear to me (kiss) My dearest friend in the world. (Goes)

*THIRD TRY

G. We've gone our separate ways for too long.
J. //~~But we've come together again.~~//
G. //~~No—~~//
J. But just now. . . .
G. Trick of memory. You know it was. Don't. . .spoil things.
J. //~~No.~~//
G. And don't be sad. You'll always be dear to me. My dearest friend in the world.

Act III, Scene 2
Richard and Virginia

V. sees her role obviously as peacemaker. But first she must pacify R's guilt. She might also think it was a storm in a teacup—R's making more of it than he needs. So perhaps she tries to make light of it. Which annoys R. So then she accuses R. of wishing the drama on himself. "It's bad for you to live under the same roof. We should have left this house long ago. You're obviously not good for each other.

Perhaps the feeling of being trapped. <u>We</u> can't afford to move. Something personal for V. needed. She means to take the initiative. Somehow.

V. (angry) I think you enjoy going at each other!
R. I meant simply to wrap him over the knuckles. But one thing led to another and suddenly we were laying his whole life out for examination.
V. (cool) And what did you find?

R. What, my dear? (surprised)

V. Did you accuse him of failure?

R. Now don't <u>you</u> start. . .

V. Richard, darling—it's the oldest thing in the world for a father to attack his son for //~~failing to~~// ^{not} live up to expectations. You two are past masters at it!

R. You're blaming me for what happened!

V. I'm not blaming either of you. I'm simply trying to put it in perspective. I'm sure painful things were said //~~on both sides. And it was unpleasant~~//— but now you must forget it.

R. Someone //~~must~~// drive the boy—he seems unable to do it for himself.

V. He's perfectly able. But he doesn't need //~~to be~~ ^{you to} ^{tell him} ~~told by you. Leave him alone. He's all right—~~ ^{He was fine when he came back from A.} ^{He had energy.} ~~he had lots of energy when he came back from America.~~ .//

R. But the wrong kind, my darling. Too frantic, too volatile.

V. I never quite know what volatile means.

R. I mean he was much too highly strung—obsessed with the glamour of money—//~~and now he's lost it all.~~ .//

V. He'll manage. //~~You see. and without your help~~// ^{If you let him.} Are you hungry?

R. What?

V. You missed lunch. (She rings for H.) I think the time has come for us to leave here. Or he must. The whole household's upset and I won't have that.

V. //~~We ought to move from here. Or he should.~~ ^{has become} ~~The two of you under the same roof//is//impossible for the rest of us.~~//

R. //~~That's what you've always wanted, really, isn't it?~~//

V. //~~No—I've been very happy. . .Oh, Hudson. . .~~//

V. I think the time's come for us to leave here. Or James must—the two of you are impossible under the same roof—you disrupt the household and _{everyone gets upset} I won't have that. (She's upset)

R. (starts to her, H. enters)

V. (recovering) Oh. . .Hudson. . .

*FURTHER NOTES

J. and G.

Forget him and marry me

What?

Marry me—it's not an eloquent proposal but—I love you, Georgina. I've always loved you. Can't think why—with Hazel was wrong. But now—I can't imagine—I mean, the future is what matters—the future for us. . . .

Row

Richard's line

At first defeatist. Waste. J.'s defense against that. R. offers support—still time—question of attitude, positive thinking. Guts. J. finds this intolerable, from his father. Counter attacks—but has no real ammunition. Sees nowhere to go. Wants to leave with open bleeding mess. Rejects conciliation.

James---------wounded tiger
Richard-------reluctant to finish him off

R. You could've married again. that would have helped.

J. How?

R. Given you happiness. //~~The care~~// responsibility
for other people.

J. Less selfish, you mean?

R. Yes, frankly. children.

J. Are children so important to a man's happiness.
I'd have thought not, judging from this conver-
sation. Anyway, if you remember, Hazel miscar-
ried.

R. Yes, yes, I know—that was very sad. But there's
still time, James. That's what I'm saying. It's up
to. . . . . .

IT IS DONE!

· · · · ·

Paul will make still other refinements.

He will drop altogether the scene where James makes his final
appeal to Georgina. In fact, he all but reverses it: Georgina, walking
into James' room as he is having his clear-out, learns that he's going
to burn the letters she wrote to him during the war; she objects;
he says Robert might see them and misunderstand; she grabs them,
saying, "They're mine! Those were happy times! Besides, I'm not
ashamed of them." They tussle over them; he grabs them back,
says, "You've made your choice," and tosses them into the fire.
Georgina turns very cool, says she must go and write Robert. "He's
miserable when he doesn't get a letter."

He will sharpen the ironies—for example, the appearances of
fresh beginnings against the reality of closed doors. He will add to
those other ghosts—Lady Marjorie, Sarah, Georgina (in the shadow
of his room)—the ghosts of old friends now in wax effigies at
Tussaud's. And he will add one last closed door—James'.

The red herring of Rose's disappearance will be counterbalanced
by a bona fide clue: the spotted Dick. For, when James offhandedly

declined the spotted Dick that Mrs. Bridges had cooked especially
for his homecoming—as for all his homecomings since he first went
away to boarding school—it was a sign given unto to all true
aficionados of the series that it was all up with James. To decline
Mrs. Bridges' spotted Dick—indeed!

The upstairs—1918.

The downstairs—1918.

Edward and his successor. (Episode 2, "A Place in the World.")

James stands for Parliament. (Episode 2, "A Place in the World.")

Daisy and Frederick. (Episode 5, "Wanted: A Good Home.")

"And thro' the field the road runs by/ To many-tower'd Camelot."
(Episode 10, "The Understudy.")

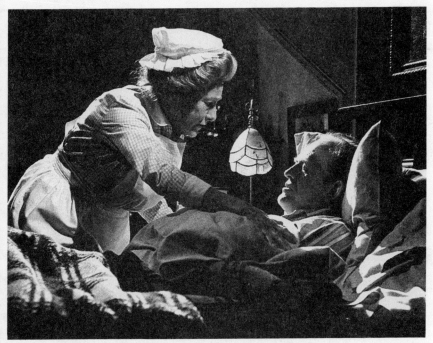

Mrs. Bridges nurses Hudson. (Episode 10, "The Understudy.")

James and Georgina in Scotland. (Episode 12, "Will Ye No Come Back Again?")

James shows his war medal. (Episode 15, "All the King's Horses.")

Mrs. Bridges, working on her masterpiece. (Episode 16, "Whither Shall I Wander?")

". . . happily ever after." (Episode 16, "Whither Shall I Wander?")

"Our revels now are ended." (Episode 16, "Whither Shall I Wander?")

PART 4

"And Which of Sarah's Pregnancies Was That, My Dear?"

Or, a guide for the baffled

containing synopses

of the fifty-five episodes

shown in the States

in the groom. So, while the bride sits upstairs, alone and unhappy, she hears from downstairs the bantering laughter of Thomas and Rose.

5. "A Pair of Exiles"   Alfred Shaughnessy
The Bellamys learn that James is in debt, is in trouble with his regiment, and is having an affair with a chorus girl. When they learn that the chorus girl is their former under-housepar-lormaid and that she is carrying James' baby . . . well, there is nothing left to do but to call in Sir Geoffrey Dillon to sort it out

6. "Whom God Hath Joined"   Jeremy Paul
Or, The Pregnant Virgin. Elizabeth comes home to Eaton Place announcing that she wants a divorce. Sir Geoffrey Dillon—of course—is called in. Adultery, he suggests? Non-consummation, she replies. In such a case, he informs her, the judge will require the testimony of an expert witness; i.e., a gynecologist.

7. "Guest of Honor"   Alfred Shaughnessy
Guess who's coming to dinner? No less than the King himself —Edward VII. Not long after the red carpet has been rolled out to the curb for him, and while the crowds are still in the street, another guest arrives, this one at the servants' entrance— unexpected, unwelcome, and in great distress.

8. "Out of the Everywhere"   Terence Brady and Charlotte Bingham
Nanny Webster, who was nanny to Lady Marjorie and to her children, is called to be nanny to the third generation—Eliza-beth's baby. While downstairs her tyrannical demands create hard feelings, upstairs Sarah alone knows that the woman is too feeble and too nearly blind to be entrusted with the care of a newborn baby.

9. "Object of Value"   Jeremy Paul
Lady Marjorie's mother, while visiting at Eaton Place, discovers
her diamond brooch is missing. When her officious lady's companion demands that the entire staff be subjected to an investigation, they are outraged. Then, as they find themselves having
to prove their innocence, the fabric of of civility and trust—so
essential where twelve people live under one roof—begins to
fray.

10. "A Special Mischief"   Anthony Skene
Elizabeth, with Rose in tow, is involved in a suffragette fracas.
Both are arrested and jailed, but when they come up in court
the next morning, a dark and handsome stranger obtains Elizabeth's release. Rose is left to endure the abusive treatment of
her jailers.

11. "The Fruits of Love"   John Hawkesworth
In order to pay the death duties on their father's estate, Lady
Marjorie's brother (the heir) is going to have to sell most of
their London property, including Number 165. Unable to raise
the money to buy it themselves, Richard and Marjorie see no
solution but to move to a more modest address—until Elizabeth
brings home her own solution. Brings him, indeed, right into
the drawing room.

12. "The Wages of Sin"   Anthony Skene
Sarah is pregnant again. "By a gentleman," she says, who
rescued her from a downpour, plied her with brandy . . . of
course, she doesn't know his name. Richard is surprised and
delighted when Thomas, the chauffeur, comes to him and tells
him he feels sorry for the poor girl and—provided he has
Richard's blessing—will offer her his hand in marriage. His
offer, like Sarah's story, seems too good to be true.

13. "A Family Gathering"   Alfred Shaughnessy
James is back from India with a fiancée who reveals her middle-
class, Army, colonial background by ordering Hudson around
as though he were an Indian houseboy. As King Edward lies
dying and the Edwardian era with it, the new order is heralded
by the arrival of Thomas and Sarah—at the *front* door—to wish
Lady Marjorie a happy birthday.

SERIES II

1. "Miss Forrest"   Alfred Shaughnessy
On a morning when Hudson has given the servants the afternoon off, James informs him he will want lunch served—in
the dining room—for himself and his father's typist. And that
he wishes Hudson to serve Richard's very best claret. Hudson
objects; James orders him; Hudson resigns; Richard says James
must apologize. Lady Marjorie says that apologizing to a servant
is out of the question. Peace is restored just before Lady Marjorie
leaves for America (on the Titanic).

2. "A House Divided"   Rosemary Anne Sisson
While Richard's typist, much to the displeasure of the staff,
takes over the running of the house, Richard's concern is with
the *cost* of running it. Knowing Richard has no money of his
own, Lady Marjorie's mother offers him a directorship in a
company in which she has substantial holdings. To accept,
Richard recognizes, would mean losing his political independence; to decline would mean losing his house.

3. "A Change of Scene"   Rosemary Anne Sisson
James, taking Hudson as his valet, visits his friend, Lord (Bunny)
Newbury, for a weekend party. Bunny is hoping that Lady
Diana Russell will say yes to marrying him; Lady Diana is
hoping for the chance to say yes to James, and the housekeeper
is hoping Hudson will say yes to taking on the job of butler
at Somerby.

4. "A Family Secret"   Alfred Shaughnessy
The downstairs, always knowing more about what goes on
upstairs than some of those involved, are not surprised when
Hazel submits her resignation to Richard. "For personal reasons," she tells him, and he believes her. The servants, however,
are not so easily deluded; the real reason, they feel sure, is
James—up to his old ways again.

5. "Rose's Pigeon"   Jeremy Paul
Rose, going to lock the back door late one night, finds Alfred,
a former footman who had run off with a German baron; hungry
and cold, he has been waiting for Rose—who he knows will
be sympathetic to any sentimental story he dreams up. As he
has expected, Rose believes his tale, hides him in a storeroom,
and brings him food. The truth is, Alfred has committed a
murder—and seems willing to commit another.

6. "Desirous of Change"   Fay Weldon
Richard has two admirers. One is a foreign adventuress who,
pretending to be an old friend of Marjorie's family—and suffering under the illusion that he is wealthy—pursues him with
matrimony in mind. The other is a new under-houseparlormaid,
who pursues him in quite a different way and with quite different illusions.

7. "Word of Honor"   Anthony Skene
A friend, wanting to ease Richard's financial plight, gives him
an investment tip, asking in return only Richard's word of
honor not to reveal the source of his information. As the friend
had said they would, the shares skyrocket. But Richard, accused
of trading on information obtained through his post in the
government, is called before a Select Committee appointed by
the Prime Minister to investigate the matter. Though it means
political ruin, Richard, bound by his word of honor, refuses
absolutely to reveal the true source of his information

8. "The Bolter"   John Hawkesworth
Hazel and James, taking Rose and Edward with them, go for
a weekend visit to a country estate. It is Hazel's first visit to
the hunt, and Edward's as well; each of them learns the arcane
ways of the country-house weekend and of the hunt, one of the
first lessons being that some of the most serious hunting takes
place not in the fields but in the bedrooms.

9. "Good Will to All Men"   Deborah Mortimer
Two lonely and frightened eighteen-year-olds join the
household—James' stepcousin, Georgina, and the new under-
houseparlormaid, Daisy. More or less overlooked in the prep-
arations for Christmas, they turn to each other for companion-
ship; on Christmas Day, at Georgina's insistence, they secretly
fill a basket with food from Mrs. Bridges' Christmas larder and
head out with it to the East End, to surprise Daisy's family.

10. "What the Footman Saw"   Jeremy Paul
Because of the goings-on Edward saw in the bedroom corridors
of the country estate, he is involved as a witness in a divorce
case. By the time Hudson and Richard explain the "ethics" of
the situation (Hudson saying that loyalty is more important
than truth), Edward is so thoroughly baffled and disillusioned
that he tells Daisy he's thinking of giving up service and joining
the Army.

11. "A Perfect Stranger"   Jeremy Paul
While Rose is riding on a tram, taking a cake to a friend of
Mrs. Bridges, an Australian sheep farmer falls into her lap and
onto her cake, ruining it. To make amends he takes her to a
tea shop to buy a replacement, invites her to take time for a
cup of tea with him . . . invites her to a *dansant*. Before long,
of course, he must be subjected to the scrutiny of the servants
at Number 165.

12. "Distant Thunder"   Alfred Shaughnessy
While Hazel convalesces from the loss of a baby by miscarriage
James consoles himself with his young stepcousin, Georgina—
leaving Richard to assume the responsibilities of comforting
and caring for Hazel and of running the house. The ensuing
frictions bring home to Richard the cruel fact that he lives at
Eaton Place only at James' sufferance.

13. "The Sudden Storm"   John Hawkesworth
Mrs. Bridges is being courted by the local fishmonger; Daisy
is being courted by Edward; Georgina, by Billy Laynton; Hazel
and James are falling out of love—and all the while, in Europe,
Germany marches.

SERIES III

1. "A Patriotic Offering"   Rosemary Anne Sisson
While James endures his bit of hell in the trenches, Eaton Place
endures a family of Belgian refugees who have arrived with
nothing intact but their lice and refuse, among other things,
the privilege of a bath. As they also speak no English, the
situation goes from bad to worse.

2. "News from the Front"   John Hawkesworth
At a small dinner party while James is home on leave, he makes
the shocking disclosure that lives are being lost for a simple
lack of guns and ammunition. Dillon, who is one of the guests,
slips the information to the press. When James' commanding
officers find out who is responsible for the slip, they have him
recalled from the front-line command. Edward, also home on
leave, uses the occasion differently—he proposes to Daisy.

3. "The Beastly Hun"   Jeremy Paul
More and more the war makes its way onto the home front.

As rumors of German atrocities spread, decent people are inflamed to indecent acts. No one of German birth is safe—not even naturalized British subjects like the Bellamys' baker, whose shop is burned and whose family is attacked.

4. "Women Shall Not Weep"   Alfred Shaughnessy
Edward and Daisy marry; Edward leaves for France; Georgina enters nurses' training; Ruby goes to work in a munitions factory—while James is forced to sit out the action behind the lines. Mrs. Bridges, who for years has maligned Ruby, now moans that she can't get along without her.

5. "Tug of War"   Rosemary Anne Sisson
Georgina, who comes home exhausted each night from scrubbing floors, nursing elderly women, and being ordered about by both the patients and the supervisors, is finally told by the matron that she has the makings of a nurse. Rose becomes a part-time conductorette on a bus, and James is allowed to return to his regiment at the front.

6. "Home Fires"   Jeremy Paul
Gregory Wilmot, Rose's Australian sheep farmer, returns—now in uniform and on leave in London after being wounded in France. Old misunderstandings are cleared up, new ones arise; but in the end Rose agrees to marry him and go to Australia with him when the war is over.

7. "If You Were the Only Girl
in the World"   John Hawkesworth
As a major offensive gets under way in France, Hazel, Georgina, Daisy, and Rose wait for news of their men. Georgina and Hazel, for James (whom Georgina has been seeing in France); Hazel, for James and for a young pilot she has been seeing in London. Downstairs, Daisy waits only for Edward; Rose, only for Gregory.

8. "The Glorious Dead"   Elizabeth Jane Howard
James returns from the front no longer the self-righteous and
self-centered young man who once had believed that the regard
for truth was more important than the regard for a person's
feelings. He has learned not only that truth is not so simple
as he had thought but also that people's feelings are more real
than he had dreamed. When he comes across the picture of
Hazel's pilot, he makes no scene; instead, he quietly invites
her out. And, for the sake of comforting Rose after Gregory's
death, he will recite those simplistic truths that she needs to
hear and that he no longer believes—about heroism and sacrifice
and pride.

9. "Another Year"   Alfred Shaughnessy
Edward, home on leave, is discovered by Richard—collapsed
on the stairs, shaken and sobbing. Richard, realizing he is
suffering from shell shock and that he is trying to hide the
fact, does for Edward what he has refused to do for his own
son—pulls strings. And what he has refused to do for an attractive young war widow, Virginia Hamilton, who has come
to the house seeking his aid. Ruby returns, a bit worse for
wear(!) as a result of her war work.

10. "The Hero's Farewell"   Rosemary Anne Sisson
Lady Pru requisitions the drawing room for a benefit theatrical
for the Red Cross. A stage is constructed, the staff is drafted
to help . . . and in the middle of a rehearsal an air raid begins.
The house suffers an indirect hit. As the debris is cleared away
the next day, a telegram arrives: James is missing in action.

11. "Missing Presumed Killed"   Jeremy Paul
James is found, alive but seriously wounded. In sympathy for
Hazel, Lady Southwold uses her influence to arrange that Richard and Hazel be allowed to take an ambulance and nurse to
the military hospital to bring him home. Georgina, who has

been nursing him at the military hospital, is appalled that James should be subjected to such a journey; but Hazel, more than a little jealous and possessive, insists.

12. "Facing Fearful Odds"   John Hawkesworth
Virginia Hamilton is back—this time imploring help for her seventeen-year-old son, who is being court-martialed for cowardice. Richard suggests that she engage Sir Geoffrey Dillon; she does, and though her son is found guilty, he is let off with a reprimand, due to his youth and to the circumstances. Edward, also suffering an attack of fear, goes AWOL.

13. "Peace out of Pain"   Alfred Shaughnessy
While James is home convalescing from his war injuries (and making everyone miserable in the bargain), the Germans begin their retreat—and the flu, its deadly advance. Even Number 165 is not immune. When the Armistice is announced, Edward, Daisy, and Ruby go out on the streets to celebrate, but Hudson, Mrs. Bridges, and Rose sit home and remember.

SERIES IV

1. "On with the Dance"   Alfred Shaughnessy
Georgina is busy with the social whirl of postwar London; James sits home, alone and depressed; Edward and Daisy have left service (he is trying to make his way in the outside world, and she is expecting a baby). Edward's place has been taken by the unscrutable Frederick, Daisy's by Lily. Into this new arrangement Richard brings his bride and her two children.

2. "A Place in the World"   Jeremy Paul
Edward, stopping in with Daisy for tea at Eaton Place, admits he has been unable to find work and that Daisy has lost her baby. When Hudson lets Edward know he has made his own

bed, the two of them have a terrible row. Nevertheless, it is Hudson who suggests to Virginia that she might take Edward on as a chauffeur and Daisy as parlormaid.

3. "Laugh a Littler Louder, Please"   Rosemary Anne Sisson
Georgina, who was saddened and matured by the war, is transformed by peace into one of those postwar phenomena known as Bright Young Things. Eaton Place (and especially Hudson) has never seen the likes of the parties she gives—costumes (scanty), gate-crashers, liquor, and a Negro jazz band. In these most unpropitious circumstances, one of Georgina's admirers insists on proposing; then, when he is turned down, he goes into a closet and shoots himself.

4. "The Joy Ride"   Alfred Shaughnessy
Virginia, spurning Richard's invitation to hear him speak in the House of Lords, accepts instead James' offer of a ride in his new airplane. As evening approaches and they have not returned, Richard begins to realize the implications of being an older man married to a younger woman who prefers adventure to long speeches.

5. "Wanted, a Good Home"   John Hawkesworth
A puppy comes to Eaton Place! Though the servants take it in their stride—it being, in fact, Rose's idea that a dog would keep Alice from being so lonely when her brother, William, leaves for boarding school—the governess is determined to get rid of it. Seeing her opportunity when Richard and Virginia leave for France, she sets about to have the dog destroyed—but she has underestimated the wiliness of the staff.

6. "An Old Flame"   John Hawkesworth
Lady Diana is chasing James again. And her lady's maid is pursuing Edward. As in the war, it is the downstairs who hold fast to the old standards, the upstairs who discard them. And

as then and always, it is Richard who must sort out the consequences—in this case, Diana's husband.

7. "Disillusion"   Alfred Shaughnessy
"Things will never be the same," declares Richard. Indeed not. Hudson has fallen in love with the under-houseparlormaid, Lily. So now it's Rose's turn to take the high moral stance. As Hudson knows only too well, it is highly improper for him to be involved with his staff; so, having violated the standards, he tenders his resignation.

8. "Such a Lovely Man"   Rosemary Anne Sisson
Virginia is not pleased when Richard asks her to entertain the wealthy Sir Guy Paynter, who Richard believes can help him win an appointment from Baldwin. The favor boomerangs when Sir Guy is smitten with Virginia, and again when—after Virginia refuses his attentions—he spitefully advises Baldwin against appointing Richard. But—more important than affairs of state—*Ruby has a suitor.*

9. "The Nine-Day Wonder"   Jeremy Paul
Eaton Place mobilizes for the General Strike. Hudson rejoins the Special Constables, to help keep peace in the streets; Georgina delivers newspapers; James drives a bus; and Frederick goes along as guard. In one of his finer moments, James averts violence when stopped by strikers intent on trouble. The strikers' side, too, makes its way into Eaton Place when Ruby's uncle and a friend, who are miners, come to the house.

10. "The Understudy" (part of the Gusset)   Jeremy Paul
Anarchy is loosed upon the household: Just before a formal dinner party for the French ambassador, Hudson suffers a heart attack. Forthwith, Mrs. Bridges collapses, while Edward and Daisy and Frederick become locked in a war of succession. Downstairs, order is restored when Rose reads the riot act to

the "jackals" who are fighting over Hudson's remains, and pushes the terrified Ruby to the cookstove. Upstairs, as always, it is Richard who takes over, calms everyone, instills confidence.

11. "Alberto"   Alfred Shaughnessy
One of Georgina's giddy and reckless friends, Lady Dolly Hale, has introduced her to a movie producer who is giving her a chance in a small part, as a French prostitute. Displeased by the publicity brewing, James makes a surprise visit to the set —just as the scantily clad Georgina has learned that the young man she is to solicit is no other than the Bellamys' footman, Frederick. James makes an unholy scene, Georgina loses her chance, and Frederick resigns as footman to pursue a newly discovered talent as "escort."

12. "Will Ye No' Come Back Again?" (part of the Gusset)
           Rosemary Anne Sisson
Georgina, James, Richard, Mrs. Bridges, Ruby, and Hudson (now recovered) go for a holiday in Scotland, in the borrowed house of a friend, where the gillie and his wife do everything in their power to discourage them from staying—including frightening Ruby out of her wits with a ghost. When Hudson calls the gillie's hand about his poaching, the ghosts disappear. For James, the holiday is a chance to be with Georgina, away from her fast friends, to make a last effort to reestablish the intimacy of the war years.

13. "Joke Over"   Rosemary Anne Sisson
On one of their all-night drinking sprees, Georgina and her friends run over and kill a country cowman. Georgina, who was driving, is brought to trial for manslaughter. She is saved from conviction only by the unexpected testimony of Robert Stockbridge, the young lord who is smitten with Georgina and, having tried and failed to dissuade her from the foolhardy drive, followed along behind them, saw the accident, and was able

to testify that no driver—drunk or sober—could have braked in time.

14. "Noblesse Oblige"
    (part of the Gusset)   John Hawkesworth
    While upstairs Georgina and Robert Stockbridge are falling in love, downstairs Ruby, tired of Mrs. Bridges' bullying, quits and takes a job as cook-general in a middle-class household. Mrs. Bridges, now having to cope with the smoking and "cater-wauling" of a disrespectful, flapperish new kitchen maid, decides to "rescue" Ruby. And indeed Ruby needs rescuing—for in middle-class households, the cook-general was often expected to take on the duties of butler, cook, maid, and footman.

15. "All the King's Horses"   Jeremy Paul
    James returns from America spreading the gospel of overnight wealth—available to rich and poor alike. Rose, intrigued, asks him to invest the thousand pounds that Gregory left her. He does—the market crashes—James is ruined—Rose's money is lost. Distraught, Rose leaves the house. Teatime comes, and no Rose; dinnertime, and still no Rose; locking-up time . . . they fear the worst. Upstairs, James, too, leaves the house, telling Hudson he is going to be staying with friends. Late in the night, two policemen come to the door. . . .

16. "Whither Shall I Wander?"   John Hawkesworth
    Robert Stockbridge has returned; his parents have consented to his marrying Georgina; and thanks to Virginia's generosity, they can have a proper wedding. But the bride and groom will not move into Number 165; so, soon after the wedding, the "For Sale" sign goes up, and the moving men carry the couch from the morning room

Drama Awards

1971	Writers Guild of Great Britain Awards	Fay Weldon, "On Trial"	Best British TV Series Script
1971	SFTA Awards	*Upstairs, Downstairs*	Best Drama Production
1972	Royal Television Society & Pye Colour TV Awards	Jean Marsh	Outstanding New Female Personality
1972	Radio Industries Club Awards	John Alderton	ITV Personality of the Year
		Upstairs, Downstairs	TV Programme of the Year
		Gordon Jackson	Best TV Actor
1973	Emmy Awards (National Academy of TV Arts & Sciences)	*Upstairs, Downstairs*	Best Drama Series
1973	American Drama Critics Circle Awards	Jean Marsh	Best Actress
1973	Writers Guild of Great Britain Awards	*Upstairs, Downstairs*	Best British TV Series Scripts
1973	American Drama Centre Awards	Jean Marsh	Best Actress
1973	SFTA Awards	John Hawkesworth	Best TV Drama Series

1974	Golden Globe Awards (Foreign Press Association)	Jean Marsh ITV Personality of the Year	Best TV Drama Series
1974	SFTA Awards	Peter Barkworth	Best Actor
1974	Writers Guild of Great Britain Awards	*Upstairs, Downstairs*	Best British TV Series Script
1974	TV Times Awards	Gordon Jackson	Most Compulsive Male TV Character
1975	Royal Television Society Awards	Gordon Jackson	Performance Award
1975	Emmy Awards (National Academy of TV Arts & Sciences)	*Upstairs, Downstairs*	Outstanding Drama Series
		Jean Marsh	Outstanding Lead Actress
		Bill Bain, "A Sudden Storm"	Outstanding Direction
1975	Variety Club of Great Britain	Gordon Jackson	ITV Personality
		Angela Baddeley	C.B.E.*
1975	Golden Globe Awards (Foreign Press Association)	*Upstairs, Downstairs*	Best TV Drama Series

*Commander of British Empire

1976	Emmy Awards (National Academy of TV Arts & Sciences)	Rex Firkin [Executive Producer] & John Hawkesworth	Best Dramatic Series
		Gordon Jackson	Best Supporting Actor
1976	PRS Ivor Novello Awards (Performing Rights Society)	"The Edwardians"	Best Theme
		Alexander Faris	Statuette
1976	TV Times Awards	Frank Finlay	Best Actor
1976	American Drama Critics Circle Awards	Rex Firkin & John Hawkesworth, *Upstairs, Downstairs*	Achievement in a Series
1977	American TV Critics Circle Awards	*Upstairs, Downstairs*	Achievement in a Series; accepted by Jean Marsh on behalf of Rex Firkin & John Hawkesworth
		Angela Baddeley	Best Actress in a Supporting Role (Posthumous)
1977	Emmy Awards (National Academy of TV Arts & Sciences)	John Hawkesworth	Outstanding Series
1978	Peabody Awards (USA)	*Upstairs, Downstairs*	

1978	Santiago, Chile	*Upstairs, Downstairs*
1977	The Queen's Jubilee Medal	Stella Ashley & Ken Payle
1979	Círculo de Críticos de Arte	*Upstairs, Downstairs*